Drama Therapy and Storymaking
in Special Education

Drama Therapy and Storymaking in Special Education

Paula Crimmens

Jessica Kingsley Publishers
London and Philadelphia

First published in 2006
by Jessica Kingsley Publishers
116 Pentonville Road
London N1 9JB, UK
and
400 Market Street, Suite 400
Philadelphia, PA 19106, USA

www.jkp.com

Library of Congress Cataloging in Publication Data
Crimmens, Paula.
Drama therapy and storymaking in special education / Paula Crimmens.
p. cm.
Includes bibliographical references.
ISBN-13: 978-1-84310-291-5 (pbk. : alk. paper)
ISBN-10: 1-84310-291-9 (pbk. : alk. paper) 1. Learning disabled children--Education. 2.
Drama--Therapeutic use. 3. Children with disabilities. I. Title.
LC4704.5.C75 2006
616.89'165--dc22

2006004551

British Library Cataloguing in Publication Data
A CIP catalogue record for this book is available from the British Library

ISBN 978 1 84310 291 5

Contents

Acknowledgments   8

Introduction   **9**
Definition of drama therapy   *9*
Drama therapy as an appropriate intervention   *11*
The use of drama therapy with people with a
        learning disability   *13*
How the book is organized   *16*

1 Getting Started   **18**
Assessing the level of the group   *18*
Working within the classroom environment   *19*
Teaching staff how to support the sessions   *21*
Creating the culture of the sessions   *23*
Physical safety   *24*

2 The Use of Traditional Stories   **27**
Why use traditional stories?   *27*
Guidelines for choosing traditional stories   *29*
Where to find appropriate stories   *32*
The use of props as aids to comprehension, participation
        and enjoyment   *32*
Allocating roles in the story   *36*
The use of song   *37*
Structuring the sessions   *38*

3	**Helping Others**	**40**
	The children and the thunder god	*41*
	The bell of Hamana	*46*
	Rata the wanderer	*50*
	The umbrella tree	*55*
4	**Dealing with Change**	**62**
	Raven and the giant who sits on the tide	*63*
	Maui and the sun	*66*
	The Windmaker	*69*
5	**Working as a Team**	**72**
	The Thunder of the Four Colours	*74*
	The bog people	*77*
	Hemi and the whale	*79*
	The healing waters	*81*
6	**Trickery and Stealing**	**85**
	King Arthur's gold	*86*
	Jack and the beanstalk	*89*
	Maui's search for fire	*93*
	Raven and the light	*96*
7	**Stories of a Special Child**	**100**
	The birth of Maui	*101*
	Momotaro	*105*
	Morning Star, Evening Star	*109*
8	**Unlikely Heroes**	**114**
	Grandmother Spider	*115*
	Yukos and the monster	*119*
	Solomon and the bee	*123*
	The first sail	*125*
9	**Competitiveness**	**129**
	Tarantula and Swift Runner	*129*
	Atalanta and the golden apples	*134*
	Paikea	*137*

10	**Trust**	**141**
	Psyche and Amor	*142*
	Vassilisa and Baba Yaga Bony Legs	*144*
	Kahakura	*149*
11	**Devising Stories: A Guide to Using Stories to Explore Themes in Everyday Life**	**154**
	Adolescent students with an intellectual disability	*154*
	Adolescent students with attentional or behavioural problems	*157*
	Students with Asperger syndrome	*162*
12	**Using a Visual Storyboard with Students with Autism**	**165**
	The storyboard	*166*
13	**Drama Therapy and Engaging the Attention of Students with an Intellectual Disability: A Research Study**	**171**
	Intellectual disability and the importance of attention	*171*
	Attention in drama therapy	*173*
	Alignment with special education literature	*174*
	Summary of literature review	*176*
	Components of the drama therapy sessions	*176*
	Measures	*180*
	Instructional procedure	*181*
	Programme support	*182*
	Results: therapist's record of sessions	*182*
	Therapist's record of changes in the four target students	*192*
	Summary	*195*
	Conclusion	*195*
	References	197
	Useful Websites	200
	Subject Index	201
	Author Index	207

Acknowledgments

I would like to acknowledge all the students and staff at the special schools where I have worked as a drama therapist. In particular, I would like to thank Heather Hedger and Lenore Lawrence at Rosehill special school for being the first to give me the opportunity and have the courage to try something new to New Zealand. I always feel so welcome in your school. Many thanks to Yvonne Lyons and Diane Hankins at Sommerville school, Laure Lamason at Oaklyn school and Judith Nicholson at Parkside school.

Many thanks to Margaret Woolgrove for all your generous help in the final workings of the book. And last but not least, thank you to my husband Tom Cooper and our two girls, Gabriel and Katie, who have suffered through long weekends of me writing stories when I could have been telling them stories.

Introduction

This book is a resource book for professionals working in special education. This includes creative therapists, teachers and teacher aides, specialist teachers for learning and behaviour plus social workers, counsellors, family therapists and others involved in the care and education of a student with special needs. Students with special education needs include those with learning and physical disabilities, behavioural and communication difficulties, sensory impairments, and medical and related conditions. This book is also written for those involved in group work with adults with a learning disability.

It places these methods of using story therapeutically within the context of drama therapy and gives practical advice on how to structure and set up sessions in a way that is compatible with the learning environment. It describes how story sessions can address issues of self-esteem and self-mastery while the group nature of the approach proves an invaluable tool for building social and communication skills.

It includes traditional stories from around the world as session material with numerous examples of their use from the author's extensive experience in special education. There is information on how to devise stories with older students that are relevant to their own experience, details of recent research into the effectiveness of drama therapy in engaging and retaining the attention of students with a learning disability, and ideas on increasing the autistic student's enjoyment and comprehension of stories with the use of visuals.i

Definition of drama therapy

Drama therapy is the use of improvisation, role-play, mime, music and movement, storytelling, masks and rituals, puppetry, theatre games and scripted drama as a therapeutic vehicle. It builds confidence, increases self-awareness, relaxation and responsibility, and operates on a variety of levels such as physical, emotional, imaginative and social. Drama therapy synthesizes many different strands of thought including anthropology, psychology, sociology, psychodrama and psychotherapy. It represents the marriage of drama and therapy, but it is not a simple addition of the two disciplines. Rather, the combination produces a third, distinct way of helping people, using appropriate elements of each area to encourage growth and development. In its focus on expression through story, drama and the physical interpretation of themes, it is unlike more traditional therapies that take a more cerebral approach.

The roots of drama therapy can be traced back to the 18th century and the performance of theatre in mental hospitals in Europe. Contemporary thinking was that acting could ameliorate the anguish of mental ill health (Casson, 1997). In the beginning of the 20th century, Freud and Jung were developing psychoanalysis, a system of viewing and working with the psyche that was to become one of the theoretical underpinnings of drama therapy (Casson, 1997). Other developments influencing drama therapy include those by Moreno, Laban and Slade. Sue Jennings, who is probably the most prolific writer and editor of drama therapy books, began working with psychiatric patients in 1964 and Marion Lindvist founded the Sesame Institute, which began the first full-time drama therapy course in 1974 (Casson, 1997).

A number of definitions of drama therapy exist. My preference as a drama therapist working in education is for those that mention learning or emphasize the practical aspects of drama therapy. Some of these are mentioned here.

> Drama therapy is action-oriented, aiming toward not only insight and emotional maturation, but also practical change... Communication skills, interpersonal dynamics, and habitual responses are all actively examined in the drama therapy session. Change is not only envisioned but literally practiced. (Emunah, 1994, p.31)

Sue Jennings (1992) also mentions change. 'Dramatherapy is the means of bringing about change in individuals and groups through direct experience of theatre art' (p.5). The British Association of Dramatherapists (BADth) define drama therapy as 'the intentional use of the healing aspects of drama and theatre within the therapeutic process. It is a method of working and playing which uses action to facilitate creativity, imagination, learning, insight and growth' (BADth, 1998).

Special education: terminology

In New Zealand, students defined as having an 'intellectual disability' (the term currently applied in educational and social policy) may be educated in mainstream settings or special schools from age 5 to 21. These students may have conditions such as Down syndrome, Autistic Spectrum Disorder and Attention Deficit Hyperactivity Disorder. Special schools may also have students with multiple handicaps. In the US, the most widely used definition is that formalized by the American Association of Mental Retardation in 1992.

> Mental retardation refers to substantial limitations in present function…and limitations in two or more of the following applicable adaptive skill areas: communication, self care, home living, social skills, community use, self direction, health and safety, functional academics, leisure and work. (Wood and Lazari 1997, pp.1–6)

I prefer the term 'learning disability' which is the term most commonly used in the UK. I will use this term in most of the book. However, the term 'intellectual disability' is used throughout Chapter 13 as it is describing a piece of research carried out in New Zealand.

Drama therapy as an appropriate intervention

Drama therapy has a number of elements that make it an appropriate or ideal intervention to use with students with special learning needs in that it does not rely exclusively on verbal and cognitive skills that may be most affected in students with a learning disability. Importantly, drama therapy uses a combination of other techniques that interact well with aspects of the student that are not impaired.

As an action orientated therapy, drama therapy appeals to the student who cannot sit still as it gives him or her something entertaining to watch and promises that a turn to perform will come. Sessions always include many opportunities for the student to get up and move.

Drama therapy uses traditional stories that capture attention with both their content, which is usually exciting, adventurous and sometimes daunting, and their structure, which is predictable and consistent. Many students with a learning disability may become anxious and more distractible in an unstructured environment. In traditional stories, there is always a beginning, middle and an end. This structure is mirrored in the structure of the session itself with its use of opening and closing songs and rituals.

Trained professionals, who are skilled in using their face, voice and movements to communicate clearly and expressively, practise drama therapy. They command attention by using modulations in their vocal tone and careful positioning of themselves in the space. Research with students with a learning disability indicates that their attention is given more readily when role models are clearly identified (Cole and Chan, 1990) and the therapist acts as or clearly nominates others to be the role model in the session.

Drama therapy uses simple, interactive tasks that the students can perform in front of the class. Students are applauded regardless of their level of participation or success in achieving a particular task and participation is never insisted on. Performance anxiety tends to increase the distractibility of students so an encouraging atmosphere is crucial to the success of the method. Students know that they can just watch and paradoxically this frees them to take greater risks than they would in a situation where compliance is expected.

Drama therapy uses dramatic conventions to increase attentiveness. These include conventions such as rehearsal and repetition, defining a space or stage, taking roles, being an audience, following cues, and giving and receiving applause. When applying drama therapy in educational settings, the sessions take place in the student's classroom and not in a theatre. However, modifications are made to make the space more conducive to paying attention.

Drama therapy is ideal for the teaching and practising of social skills with children with cognitive and communication impairments. Social inter-action depends on good communication skills (Craig, 1993) and cognition, both being areas that are likely to be impaired in children with a disability. These impairments make the acquisition of social skills problematic as well as making it more likely that these children will be excluded from normal peer interactions or play where these complex skills are more usually developed. Social competence has been defined as displaying appropriate social behaviour and the ability to resolve conflict in an acceptable manner (Antia and Kreimeyer, 1992; Berk, 1996), being effective in achieving social goals (Rose-Krasnor, 1985), and having the ability to respond with an appropriate behaviour at an appropriate time that is within the social context (Ross and Rogers, 1990). Little wonder Krakow and Kopp (1982) remark that participating in a social situation and responding to social cues is a par-ticular challenge for children with a disability! Friendship formation is a learned behaviour through use of social skills (Csoti, 2000). Richard Lavoie

(1994) has expressed concern that children with a learning disability are without friendships, seeing their isolation as being caused by immature and unpredictable behaviour that is often misinterpreted by peers and adults. Schumaker and Deshler (1995) agree but suggest that with specialized coaching these children can learn multifaceted social behaviours. Kymissus (2001) (cited in Geldard and Geldard, 2001) supports Corey and Corey (1997) in suggesting that group settings are ideal for interventions that address interrelationships in childhood. As a group-based therapy, drama therapy provides a microcosm of a world that may be too bewildering, over-stimulating and verbal for the learning disabled child to navigate. Poor impulse control impacts on social behaviour and the drama therapy session works to improve this – even just the process of sitting on a chair and awaiting your turn goes some way to teaching impulse control. The use of the repetitious phrase 'everyone has a turn who wants a turn' reassures and encourages the child to wait his turn, as his turn will come.

The use of drama therapy with people with a learning disability

Several influential practitioners did their seminal work in the area of learning disability. For instance, Marion Lindvist pioneered the Sesame approach of movement and drama therapy in her work with autistic students. Writing here of the benefits of drama therapy she says,

> It seems clear that it can be used as a means of communication, for developing relationships, increasing body awareness, and for minimising stereotypes... It can give satisfaction to the doer, and encourage verbalisation as well as group awareness and a sense of sharing a creative experience. It can also increase confidence (cited in Shatner and Courtney, 1977, p.54).

Sue Jennings, who wrote *Remedial Drama* in 1973, included chapters on 'Drama and the Backward Child' and 'Drama with the Severely Subnormal and Multiply Handicapped'. It is an informative and practical book and communicated the joy and satisfaction of working creatively with this client group. However, more recently, Anna Chesner (1995) has written that 'The specialist use of drama therapy for people with learning disabilities does not play a central role in the professional training courses in the UK and even runs the risk of being placed on the margins of clinical drama therapy work'

(p.5). Chesner (1995) suggests that although drama therapy in the UK originally had its roots in work with people with a learning disability, it quickly
expanded into other areas by the very nature of its flexibility and appropriateness for a number of different client groups.

Marilyn Richman details the effectiveness of creative drama with
children with Attention Deficit Hyperactivity Disorder (ADHD). She
outlines the characteristics of ADHD in terms of deficits in perception,
cognition, language skills, memory, behaviour and social and emotional
development. Richman then identifies aspects of creative drama that are
effective in the treatment of these deficits. These include the use of games to
focus observation and control, consistent structure, problem solving and
praise for appropriate skills (M. Richman, personal communication, 3 May
2004).

The use of other creative therapies with students with a learning disability

Aldridge, Gustorff and Neugebauer (1995) note that the music therapy
approach of Nordoff and Robbins had its origins in work with learning
disabled children. The authors describe how and in what ways 'music
therapy would seem to be an ideal medium' (1995, p.192) for addressing
issues of developmental delay, particularly communication and proprioception. They carried out research where results indicated that participation
in improvised creative music therapy facilitated development in children
whose development was delayed. The changes were largely in the areas of
communication and language development.

Special education teachers Lyons and Tropea detailed the benefits of
using art. They wrote that this could be beneficial in several ways, such as
'the release of tension and venting of emotions as well as building tolerance
to frustration, addressing issues of body image and *remediation of learning difficulties*' (1987, p.245, my emphasis).

Wengrower (2001) stressed the holistic nature of the creative therapies.
'Therapy through expression and creativity employs one's entire personality,
employing emotional, cognitive and motorical skills; it therefore meets the
multi-dimensional needs of special education pupils, such as children with
learning disabilities, mental impairments, and/or emotional and behavioural
problems' (p.114).

One of the most common themes across these approaches appears to be
the acquisition of social skills that can be taught and practised in a safe group
environment. For instance, Berrol states that 'dance therapy is used [in] the

development of body scheme, creativity and motoric awareness and control. Just as important, especially for these pupils, is the focus on socialization skills via activities that require group cooperation' (1989, p.84).

Improving communication skills and providing alternative means to communication were other major benefits attributed to the use of creative therapies generally. 'Music therapy encourages children without language to communicate and has developed a significant place in the treatment of mental handicap in children' (Aldridge *et al.*, 1995, p.190). Roth and Rowland also emphasized the importance of the creative therapies in providing alternative means of communication for the nonverbal child. 'For the non verbal child, both play therapy and art therapy offer a special form of self expression that is meaningful' (1980, p.19).

Another common theme is the identification of emotional and behavioural problems in students with a learning disability and as a corollary to that, the effectiveness of using creative therapies as part of a treatment programme. Berrol identified her client group as 'possessing neurological disorders overlaid with emotional problems' (1989, p.85). She believed the behaviour problems obstructed learning. 'Art therapy and play therapy aid in decreasing disturbed behaviour. With a decrease in disturbed behaviour, the child has a better opportunity to increase his intellectual functioning and adaptive behaviour within the limitations of his retardation' (Roth and Rowland, 1980, p. 20). Developmentally delayed children were 'more likely to experience rejection when they fail to meet standards of expectations associated with their chronological age. This rejection can lead to behavioural disturbances' (Aldridge *et al.* 1995, p.190).

Most creative therapists focus on social skills development, acquisition of language or addressing the emotional issues in being a child with a learning disability. 'Through the medium of drama, a child can explore the physical and social environment, address past and current emotional issues as well as concerns for the future, create a role repertoire, and achieve real satisfaction from imaginary events' (O'Doherty, 1989, p.177). Susan O'Doherty goes as far as seeing the lack of spontaneity and imaginative skills of children with Down syndrome to be 'affective rather than cognitive'(1989, p.172). She details at some length the circumstances surrounding the birth of a child with Down syndrome that would provide ample material with which to work. These included 'feeding disorders, parental grief and rejection, separation from parents due to hospitalization, and the restrictions inherent in early schooling' (p.171). She also persuasively argues the case for drama therapy and play therapy as effective tools to 'reconstruct and recast these circumstances in a positive light' (p.171).

> Expression through art is an activity that has social value and is socially acceptable. Therefore, therapy based on such activity is less stigma-tizing. It allows the integration of the child's unimpaired aspects while he/she is undergoing therapy. Thus, he/she may work on his weak-nesses and ways of coping with them, while at the same time uncovering his/her strengths. This has a positive effect on self-image. (Wengrower, 2001, p.114)

Here the author is referring specifically to the use of creative therapies in mainstream schools but it is a belief equally pertinent to special schools.

Problems with proprioception are very common in children with a learning disability. Proprioception is a term used to describe awareness of body position. Drama and dance/movement therapy are two very useful ways of addressing and helping to rectify this problem. It is interesting that it is Aldridge, Gustorff and Neugebauer – the music therapists – who refer to it directly and in reference to it say ' Active music therapy would seem to be an ideal medium for encouraging purposeful controlled movement in a time structure that is formed yet flexible' (1995, p.192). However, Berrol seems to be talking about the same thing when she refers to activities that 'stimulate the tactile and vestibular systems' (1989, p.87), while Anna Chesner (1995) suggests activities and exercises which would be very beneficial in the treatment of problems of proprioception but never uses the actual term.

How the book is organized

Chapter 1 contains a description of the practical aspects involved in running sessions in special schools. Chapter 2 gives guidelines on using traditional stories with younger students and older students with a range of abilities while Chapters 3 to 10 are grouped around stories which address different aspects of social, communication and values education, an analysis of their themes and practical ideas for how to use them with students. In Chapter 11, I describe ways to devise stories with older students who are developmentally adolescents and who have the cognitive ability to explore issues relevant to their lives. Chapter 12 describes how to create storyboard stories to increase understanding in students with autism. Chapter 13 contains a description of a research study carried out to assess the levels of engagement in students with a learning disability.

Note

Throughout the book, therapists and support staff are referred to as 'she'; students are referred to as 'he', unless they are clearly female. The names of all students have been changed to protect their identities.

1

Getting Started

Assessing the level of the group

A first step is to assess the group in terms of individual and group strengths. The more you know about individuals in the group, their likes and dislikes, their strengths and areas they need to develop, the better. Any other information you can get from other members of a multi-disciplinary team, for example, the physiotherapist, the speech and language therapist and the occupational therapist, can also be useful. However, people you know well can still react surprisingly in the creative atmosphere of the group, while groups about which you have very little information can develop well if you take things slowly and sensitively. Generally, the more disabled the students, the more support and input will need to be provided and the less spontaneity and initiative can be expected to arise naturally from the group.

Next, it can be useful to assess the level of the group in terms of the developmental age of the students rather than their chronological age. For example, I had a class of 7-year-olds who were developmentally, on many levels, no older than 18 months. They toddled or bottom shuffled, they were pre-verbal, they sucked their thumbs and one student put everything into his mouth immediately and explored it with his tongue. What we did in this group was vastly different to what I would do in groups of students who are developmentally 6 or 7 years old. This group of 7-year-olds was developmentally a group of infants and their needs were very fundamental. One of the classroom goals was to teach the students how to sit on chairs as part of an overall programme of teaching them appropriate school behaviour. The drama therapy sessions alternated short periods on chairs with activities that acknowledged their actual developmental needs. This is what Sue Jennings refers to on her 'developmental play paradigm' as the embodiment stage (Jennings, 1990), and Erikson refers to as 'autocosmic play' (1995). The activities involved the physical closeness of cuddling, singing and rocking as well as opportunities to explore the senses and the immediate environment while recognizing the infant's pattern of needing to alternate exploration with reassurance.

Sometimes students who are chronologically teenagers are clearly pre-pubescent in their thinking, emotional maturity and interests. They will still enjoy the traditional stories and many of the activities that appeal to the younger students. However, for students who are adolescent and who may feel uncomfortable with some of the more childlike features of the session, there is a way of working with story that I will describe in Chapter 11.

Pitching the session at the right level for the students in the group takes experience and sometimes trial and error. As we build a relationship with individuals, we can be influenced by what we observe that they enjoy and if the atmosphere is playful, flexible and encouraging, everyone, both staff and students, can feel confident about expressing more of whom they are.

Working within the classroom environment

You may be running the group in a classroom, and this has a number of advantages and disadvantages. The first advantage is that in the familiar learning environment the students are less likely to be distracted, and the environment serves as a prompt for attentiveness. You may want to cordon off specific areas of the room and position yourself so that there is nothing too distracting behind you. A large space is not necessarily a good thing as it is easier to 'lose' students. If you find yourself in the gym or a large room, you can use room dividers to make the space more manageable. When I first began working in special schools, I wanted the students to experience more of the general space in the room, to encourage greater freedoms and spontaneity. At this stage, I conceived of what I was doing as an alternative to what was being offered in the classroom the rest of the time. I took students off their chairs and onto the floor and although I began the session with the group sitting in a semi-circle I tried to move out from it into the rest of the room, going on journeys and adventures. It did not take long for me to adapt my ideas and I soon learned that the structure offered by the simple use of the chair was invaluable. While the children have their own chairs, they have territory or delineated space that they do not have to defend. While on the floor many students began scratching, fighting with one another, and became clearly distracted by the other students' close physical proximity. On the floor, some students would recline or lie down and stop paying attention, as if they were relaxing at home in front of the TV, whereas sitting on the chair reminded the student to pay attention. However, with profoundly disabled students, I try to get them out of their chairs and onto the floor supported by staff as much as possible. Many of these students spend a lot of time in chairs, which allow them to doze easily, whereas sitting supported on the floor demands far more of their muscles and gives the student lots of good body contact. Consequently, they tend to be more alert.

The second thing I learned was that any movement away from the semi-circle shape facing me caused a number of students to lose attention completely. They would become distracted by other objects in the room, return to stereotypic behaviours or generally drift off. I developed a way of working that complemented and supported the classroom aims of sitting in chairs, listening, staying on task and paying attention. Now most of the action takes place within the delineated space of the semi-circle with the students leaving their chair to perform and then returning to their chair. This doesn't mean I abandon exploring the wider, general space in the room. I just limit it and avoid it on days when students seem particularly distractible. In some cases, I provide structure by giving students a rope or long piece of fabric to hold on to while they explore the space or use a thread drawn around the furniture in the room for them to follow.

One of the disadvantages of running the session in the classroom is that other people may not be aware that something special is going on which needs to be uninterrupted. It is very common in classrooms for people to wander in and out, speak to the teacher or withdraw a student. When I first began working in special schools, I was the only person who was running a group activity where I aimed to engage the attention of the whole group. Often there are other professionals employed in the care of the student such as occupational therapists and physiotherapists, whose job is to work with individual students. They may have no idea what you are trying to achieve and quite innocently come into the classroom and withdraw a student. It is worthwhile taking the time to explain some of your goals and asking people not to come into the classroom unless they absolutely have to and to avoid withdrawing a student before the end of the session. I often explain that in drama therapy, we use structured sessions to bring about a number of aims and objectives, one of which is to encourage absorption in the students. Absorption is a state where true learning and therapy can take place. It is often observed in 'normal' childhood development but may be very rare in some children and which further compounds their learning difficulties. In children whose attention span is short, the therapist and support staff work hard to continually redirect the child's attention to a point where creativity is focused, roles are chosen and enacted and the child is taking part in the story in a very concentrated way. Everything in the session promotes this absorption, from the ritualized beginnings and endings, to the use of the circle, the repetition of key phrases in the story, and the careful choice of props and objects. The formal timetabling of drama therapy and the freeing up of staff to assist the drama therapist all support this process.

I have found that some staff not directly involved in the drama really appreciate the opportunity to sit in on a session. When this is the case, I encourage them to participate rather than just observe. They then get the chance to experience first hand what it is like to become absorbed in the story and how easily an interruption destroys the atmosphere you have carefully built up.

Teaching staff how to support the sessions

If you are a teacher using this book with your own class, you may already be familiar with both the students and your support staff. Two things may be a challenge for you. One is the need to set aside expectations that students will meet educational goals and learning outcomes. The paradox is that we are then free to notice the other achievements the student is making. I am not saying that there will not be educational outcomes. There will. Just do not focus on them. The second challenge may be to be more playful and relaxed with your students. Your efforts will be rewarded by how delighted the students are to see another aspect of their teacher.

If you are coming into someone else's classroom, you need to appreciate how important the teacher is to the emotional security of the students in the class. Simply put, the more involved the teacher, the better the session. The students will look to the teacher for reassurance and if they see her enthusiasm, they will take their cue from her. They will look to her for leadership and when they see her defer to you, they will accept your leadership. This is not so important once the group is established, but at least initially, it is very important to have the enthusiastic participation of the teacher. If the teacher is enthusiastic about the benefits for her students but uncomfortable about participating in the session, then encourage her to use the time as she sees fit and focus more on getting support staff on board.

The main point I am making is that it is not possible or indeed preferable to run a group solo. Support might comprise one additional staff member in a group of older students who are highly functioning, or one-on-one staff support in a class of students with multiple disabilities.

Although it can be great to have an enthusiastic staff member, it is important that they do not take the attention away from the students. I have therefore identified five major ways in which staff can support you to run the sessions. These are redirecting attention, helping a student to do a task (either literally hand over hand or encouraging), discouraging unacceptable behaviour, modelling and playing a role. The first three ways may already be familiar to the staff member but the last two require further explanation. Most of the students in this setting are primarily visual: they learn through watching rather than through listening to verbal instructions. The notable exceptions to this are students with a nonverbal learning disability who learn best through step-by-step verbal or written instructions. Modelling comprises modelling a task you want the students to perform, or appropriate behaviour like looking attentive and enthusiastic. It may also involve elements of role-play. For example, the staff member may model chopping down a tree while in role as the woodcutter. A member of staff who is willing to role-play is a huge asset and students are often delighted to see this familiar person transforming themselves for the sake of the story. For staff members who are unfamiliar with this way of working some reassurance may be needed. I often say, 'Don't worry. I'll tell you exactly what to do.' Some staff are naturally dramatic and prove fun and exciting to work with. Some staff are much loved by the students and prove invaluable playing roles where you want to excite the students' sympathy and concern.

Often staff are keen to help when they understand some of the rationale behind what you are doing but you also need to be clear about what you do not want. For example, you want students to volunteer rather than be persuaded or coerced. You need to be prepared to intervene if staff are persuading or coercing the students. Initially, staff may be anxious that their students 'perform' and they need to understand that in the early days of a group it is enough that the students sit in their chairs and watch what is happening. Staff may need to be reminded that the emphasis is on the process rather than the product. You may need to talk to them about the importance of offering choice even when the student may need a great deal of support in order to make the choice. To illustrate: in a profoundly disabled group, the staff member stands before a student in a wheelchair with two brightly coloured fabrics in her hands. 'Now then, Paul,' she says, 'which one of these do you like?' She offers the red one and watches Paul's reaction.

'Ah, Paul, I see you looking at the red one. What about this one?' She removes the red one and offers the green one. Paul's pupils dilate as he looks at the green fabric. He tracks and follows it as the staff member moves it around. 'Oh, Paul, good looking. I think you really like the green one!' She places the fabric gently around his shoulders.

Violet Oaklander, in referring to hyperactive children, says,

> Making choices requires a sense of self; one must tune into one's thinking and feeling functions in order to make a decision. Taking responsibility for one's choice is a learning experience. In our zeal to create limits and structure…we often neglect to give them enough experience with the strengthening process of making choices. (Oaklander, 1978, p.230)

Make staff familiar with the catchphrases in the session such as 'Everybody has a turn who wants a turn.' If you want students to learn how to take turns they need to know that if they sit nicely and wait they will get their turn. If it means that you jettison what you had planned for the rest of the session so that everyone can have a turn, say, at a new activity which you had offered but were not sure would go down well, then so be it. Difficulties arise when the nature of the class is such that students who have already had their turn start to get restless. Balancing the needs of the individuals in the group is an art and one that demands much creativity on the part of the facilitator. The catchphrase 'Everybody has a turn who wants a turn' also leaves space for the student who doesn't want to have a turn.

Creating the culture of the sessions

The culture that you are trying to create in the sessions is one of cooperation, mutual understanding, helpfulness and sensitivity towards others. These are themes explored in the stories, implicit in the stories, modelled, and practised in the sessions by all. The vital prerequisite for the cultivation of these qualities is safety.

> In terms of therapeutic process, the drama therapist works towards giving the client an experience of safety. The therapeutic environment is one where a client may learn to trust. This trust takes the form of a trust of the space, of the therapist, of the group in the case of group dramatherapy and of the self. If the therapy space feels insecure, or the presence of the therapist is unreliable, it is difficult for the client to take in the nourishment that is offered. (Chesner, 1995, p.8)

It's the facilitator's job to ensure the safety of the group. There are two aspects to safety: physical safety – that a student is confident that they will not be hit or attacked in a session, and emotional safety – that they will not be laughed at or put down or made to feel bad.

'The working ethos of the dramatherapy group is one which values the creative contribution and ability of each person, rather than focusing exclusively on what is dysfunctional or disabled' (Chesner, 1995, p.131).

Physical safety

Any kind of hitting out, kicking or biting is unacceptable and the session cannot function with someone who is going to do that. A safe group, where people can move around and interact with one another without fear of being hurt, is essential. I will often interpret the aggression in terms of whether it is a reactive or a deliberate strategy although in both cases the response is approximately the same.

For many students, close physical contact with others is potentially distressing and sometimes alarming. Some students abhor loud noises, so sessions which include percussion or singing disturb them. In these cases, the hitting is a defensive action and what the student needs is distance and time to come back to him, calm down and prepare to return to the group. This process may only take a few moments. I will organize his chair to be withdrawn from the circle so that he can see what is happening but experience some distance from other students. It is immediately apparent that this strategy has been the appropriate one when you can see the student calm down and sit quite happily. He may need to be accompanied by a staff member.

Support staff may need to be taught how to use this strategy and to explain that it is not a punishment. You may need to teach them to be very matter of fact about withdrawing a student to sit on the chair and monitor their demeanour to assess whether they are ready to rejoin the group or whether it would be better for them to remain on the chair participating from a distance. You emphasize that there is no shame involved in this – just a recognition that for some students such close physical proximity with others combined with a lot of sensory stimulation may prove to be too rich a brew. You have provided something which the student in the moment could probably not articulate for himself: space. Instruct the support staff to check with the student every couple of minutes whether he wants to return to the circle and tell them not to apply any pressure. This is an important part of building within a student the confidence that his needs will not be overridden within a group situation. Often the reason why autistic students avoid group activities is that they are not allowed to take the space they need in order to tolerate close physical proximity to other people.

There is also the aggression that is habitual and designed to get a particular response from adults, usually attention. The time-out chair is a useful way of not rewarding unacceptable behaviour with attention. The next step is to teach the student that the appropriate way of getting the attention he craves is within the semi-circle, participating in the activities. Usually the student who uses hitting out as attention seeking will be very keen to rejoin the group. Praise and affirm his ability to be part of the group as soon as possible.

Having said this, there are still occasions where the only solution is to exclude the student from sessions. In my experience, this has been rare, particularly if the student appears to be benefiting and enjoying drama. In one instance, the student was new to the school and extremely high functioning. However, he was also almost compulsively aggressive towards others. The teacher, in consultation with the family and other members of staff, had devised a behavioral programme that involved ignoring and not reacting to these very common outbursts. The aim was to avoid positively or negatively reinforcing the behaviour. Over time, the incidences seemed to be decreasing. However, even with a staff member sitting beside this student throughout drama it proved impossible to protect others in the class from his violence because of the high level of interaction and movement combined with the student's own determination to inflict harm. In the end, I had to ask for the student to be excluded as I could see that examples of nipping and biting were flaring up amongst the other students, which was understandable when they felt unsafe.

If the emotional safety of the group is being compromised by verbal put-downs you may have to use your knowledge of the group to decide whether a simple catchphrase like 'We don't have put-downs in drama' is sufficient followed by time out if continued. This is often all that is needed with younger students. However, you may decide that bullying and put-downs are what you want to explore in drama, in which case you may want to utilize some of the ideas in Chapter 11 on devising stories. Whatever form the challenges take it is the responsibility of the facilitator to make an appropriate intervention and reaffirm the boundaries. If she does not the group will begin to feel unsafe and lack of safety in a group is characterized by compliance or disruptiveness. The sessions will also be marked by a lack of genuine spontaneity and creativity and the students will cease to function therapeutically.

Confidence is another important part of making a group safe: confidence in one's skills, knowledge base and ability to hold the group. Bernie Warren says 'Only when leaders create a positive and self confident atmosphere can the members of a group start to feel secure enough to express themselves' (1993, p.7). It helps one's confidence to have spent time thinking about and planning the session, and making sure that you have all the props you need.

Confidence in the group members is also important. I make a point of demonstrating my confidence in the good will of members of the group and that they can all be trusted to act sensitively. One example is me role-playing the tree that the student 'chops' down with a plastic axe. I always approach the role with absolute confidence that the student will play his part (as opposed to using the opportunity to hurt me). Students have a way of adapting their behaviour to meet our expectations and expecting gentleness and awareness of others has a powerful effect.

> The therapeutic process is an invitation to be vulnerable, to be open to feelings and contact. The client needs to know that the human condition is a shared one and the vulnerability is not all on his or her side. If the therapist can trust the client to be appropriate and sensitive in this situation the client's own confidence and self-esteem is nurtured. (Chesner, 1995, p.41)

2

The Use of Traditional Stories

Why use traditional stories?

There are several reasons for using traditional stories as the basis of the session.

1. They provide an existing structure for both the student and facilitator. They have a recognizable beginning, middle and end.

   The structure of the myth or old tale provides the safe passage, enabling us to negotiate rough seas, hear the siren's song, meet the three headed dog and return, safe, sometimes stirred or even uncomfortable, but with the possibility of greater awareness. (Watts, 1985, p.6)

2. They provide a huge resource for the facilitator. Folk tales, fairy tales and myths form a vast storehouse of material that is very easy to access. What this book aims to do is give guidelines on how to sift through, discriminate and choose what best reflects the needs of your students.

3. We can choose traditional stories that mirror aspects of individuals in the group and thus affirm their experiences. This includes stories where the hero is abandoned at birth ('The birth of Maui', Chapter 7: Stories of a Special Child), assumed unlikely to succeed ('Grandmother spider', Chapter 8: Unlikely Heroes), or jealous of a popular friend ('Tarantula and Swift Runner', Chapter 9: Competitiveness). A student's cultural identity may also be affirmed by the use of a story from his own culture.

4. Traditional stories address issues in an indirect way, as they are firmly located in the far away and long ago. This is of particular relevance to professionals working creatively with students where they are concerned about accessing unconscious material which they do not feel qualified to deal with. Working with myth and

traditional stories performs the function of distancing and providing emotional safety. The student can choose to identify with the characters and their dilemmas or not. In this way, drama therapy is a distinct departure from psychodrama. Kim Dent-Brown writes:

> Setting the story in a far distant time and place, with characters who are utterly different from the patient and those around them provides a degree of distance. This means that themes and relationships can be seen at a process level, rather than being always dictated by content. (1999, p.11)

5. Traditional stories are conduits for education about values and express complex issues in a way that most students can understand. Stories are chosen which affirm the importance of sharing and cooperating and present individual qualities as enhancing and contributing to the community. Many of the stories I use come from cultures that adopt a collective model where the group is paramount and individual preferences are subsumed for the good of the community. They are also characterized by a mutually beneficial relationship between humans and their environment. Other cultures exposed to Western philosophical influences developed a 'humanistic' way of looking at the world where people perceive themselves as intrinsically superior to animals and plants which consequently changes their relationship to their environment. These ideas arose out of Classical Greek philosophy, were refined under early Christianity and were further developed by the French philosopher Descartes in what is known as Cartesian dualism where concepts such as mind and body, spirit and matter are split and frequently opposed. These ideas, argues Tuhiwai-Smith in her book *Decolonizing Methodologies, Research and Indigenous Peoples,* became the Western concept of reality out of which developed the individual as the basic unit of society. In drama therapy, we are trying to promote a sense of one's own individuality while encouraging an awareness of the needs of others. The traditional stories in this book describe a collective model and by exploring them in a group students are encouraged to develop a greater sense of others. Within the session, we are asking students to make choices, take initiative, and increase body awareness, all of which are ways of developing vital self-awareness and a stronger sense of self.

With which groups do we use traditional stories?

- With groups of developmentally and chronologically younger students; traditional stories employ a simple structure and narrative, which can teach students about the consequences of actions and help demystify complexities of human behaviour and emotions.

- With any groups where students need the additional distancing of the 'long ago and far away' aspect of the traditional story. Occasionally, in special schools, I have had students with a dual diagnosis of a learning disability and Post Traumatic Stress Disorder. In these cases it is important to be aware of the possibility of triggering past trauma and to avoid scenarios close to the students' own experience.

With which groups do we devise stories?

- With groups of students who are developmentally older, i.e. adolescent.

- Also for students with nonverbal disabilities like Asperger where an inability to read nonverbal cues and consequent inappropriate responses impact negatively on peer relationships.

- With students with behavioural difficulties like conduct disorder and ADHD.

For more information on the use of devised stories, see Chapter 11.

Guidelines for choosing traditional stories

The first guideline for choosing a traditional story is that there is plenty of action. A story with too much description and dialogue is not suitable. The reason for this is the nature of the client group. A learning disability generally makes words problematic. It is where drama's power of 'show me' rather than 'tell me' comes into its own. The active nature of the sessions is one many teachers appreciate as their students may be relatively inactive due to a variety of reasons which increase as they get older. Sometimes the presence of a physical disability means that historically these students have been discouraged from moving due to anxiety for their safety. Sometimes the students move too much: they may be unable to sit still and the active nature of the group is very attractive for them.

The six-stage story

The action in the story is often constellated around a challenge or task. A model I find very useful in analysing stories is an assessment tool devised by Israeli drama therapist Mooli Lahad (p.150, cited in Jennings, 1992). It was originally formulated for work with children in times of distress to help them articulate and express their experience and was envisioned as a drawing exercise with pen and paper. However, the six stages Lahad describes provide a very neat outline of almost all of the stories I use in work with this client group. The model takes as its starting point the reality of challenge as part of an overall experience of life. What determines success is the balance between obstacles and supports. With sufficient support, we can meet and achieve our goals and move on. With too many obstacles we can flounder. The model has similarities with what Vygotsky termed the proximal zone (1978). This is the place between the students' level of competency and new learning, and support that can help the student move from one to the other. The knack is to set up goals that are attainable with effort. If the obstacles are too great and the supports insufficient the student may feel discouraged. At the same time, if the activity is too easy and requires little effort, the student can become complacent and bored.

The six stages of the story structure are as follows:

1. Who is the character, animal, creature or thing that this story is about?

2. What is his or her task or goal?

3. What or who are his or her supports? This can be external, as in the case of people or animals, or internal, as in the case of personal attributes like courage or steadfastness.

4. What are the obstacles, the things that stand in the way of achieving the goal?

5. How is the goal achieved?

6. What happens next? What is the outcome? Is that the end of the story or does it carry on?

Using this model, for example, with the story of Maui and the sun, described in Chapter 4, we can see that Maui is the hero and his goal is to slow down the sun. His brothers and his own courage and obstinate refusal to accept limitations support him. The obstacles are initially his brothers' reluctance to participate in the quest and then the sheer power and might of the sun. He achieves his goal by enlisting the support of his brothers, travelling at the right time of day, planning, waiting, constructing a special net and refusing to give in. The outcome is a much better quality of life for everyone.

Opportunities for student participation and interaction: the tasks

Tasks are the breakdown of parts of the story that a student can do in front of an audience (the rest of the class) after modelling by me or a member of staff. They often comprise a sequence of simple, connected actions. Sequences are often problematic for students with an intellectual disability. Sequences usually fall naturally into three stages. They require attention and the ability to remember the sequence correctly. The tasks involve rehearsal and repetition. As each student takes a turn, the students watching have another chance to learn the sequence. I choose the first student to attempt the task after I have modelled it carefully. I look for a student who I think is most likely to copy the task accurately as other students tend to copy the person they have watched directly before they have a turn. If a student leaves out a stage in the sequence or jumps a stage, I ask him to sit down and try again at the end. Everybody who wants a turn has a turn and extra support is given when needed. The completion of the task earns applause from the audience. Obviously, the more vivid the task the easier it is for the students to grasp and copy. Here are some examples of sequences from stories in this book.

Momotaro The old woman goes down to the river to wash her clothes. The task is to wash the clothes in the river (symbolized by a long piece of blue fabric). The sequence is as follows:

1. Take the washing out of the basket and rub it vigorously in the 'water'.

2. Hold washing loosely in hands and rinse in the 'water'.

3. Grasp the washing in two hands and wring out the 'water' saying, 'squeeze'.

The children and the thunder god The children and the old man are working in the fields. The task is to get ready for the thunder. The sequence is as follows:

1. With an outstretched palm, the old man growls at the children, 'Get in the house,' and jerks his thumb behind him.

2. He goes and gets his chopper and stands ready.

3. He cups his ear and says, 'I hear thunder,' in an ominous voice.

A task may be a purely physical undertaking like chopping with the axe or it may involve some characterization like pretending to be the woodcutter and miming being hot and tired. In this way the task may lead on to students beginning to role-play.

Where to find appropriate stories

There are many places to access stories but the first place to look is within oneself. When we allow ourselves to think about it, we discover that we have a plethora of stories at our fingertips and more and more emerge as we let ourselves think and remember. We discover that we have a huge amount of potential material without having to consult a single book (let alone the vast number of resources available to us on the internet – a search engine will throw up thousands of relevant websites; see Useful Websites, p.200 for details). When we make this realization, it is very exciting because we can begin to take ownership of the resource and begin to become more confident in both using and adapting stories to suit our purposes. Pooling stories with friends and colleagues can stimulate recollections and increase our enjoyment of stories. Libraries are a good resource either for books themselves (in the mythology, anthroplogy or the children's section) or for details of storytelling events and festivals.

The use of props as aids to comprehension, participation and enjoyment

When cognitive abilities are impaired, the ability to imagine is compromised. We become literal and need concreteness in order to understand. A story is an abstract concept couched in language. In order to make it accessible for students with impaired cognitive abilities we have to include 'props' which assist understanding and stimulate participation. Props are never chosen randomly. They must always link with the story and are used selectively and economically. It is usually better to have two or three well-chosen props that students must share and wait to use than a whole bag full of props which lose their significance and dramatic intensity.

My most commonly used props
FABRICS

Lycra

The most versatile prop I use is a three-metre piece of lycra. Lycra is visually engaging, comes in a variety of colours and is stretchy and incredibly strong. I have used it to bear the weight of heavy students on occasion. (Because fabric weights and strength vary, it is important to test the fabric before using.) It also washes easily. It can be stretched out like a parachute and have things bounced on it like balls, balloons or bubbles. It can be used to hold someone like a hammock. Students love to crawl under it. It can be used as a rope or a bag. Blue lycra can be the sea, sky or a river while green makes a good forest canopy.

The tube

The next most versatile prop is a three-metre length of jersey material that comes in a tube and is very inexpensive. I hit on this idea when I was looking for ways to facilitate crawling and discovered that the nylon tunnels which you can buy are expensive and can be hard on hands and knees. The tube can be pulled shorter to make it easier for a nervous student to crawl through. I hold it at one end and ask a staff member to hold the other and look through to encourage students. Usually most students are keen to have a go and want to have a number of turns. Some students really like the sensation of being in the tube and don't want to come out the other end. If I think this is going to happen, I usually have two tubes available and I can let that student have a rest within the relative security of one while I carry on using the other for the rest of the class to crawl through. The tube has a reasonable amount of flexibility. I have certainly managed to draw it down and over someone sitting in a wheelchair. The tube can be used as a rope or a hiding place and commonly is worn by whoever is playing a tree!

Fabrics can be used to create quick costumes and stage effects, for example a piece of white netting that is covered in gold stars. I look for bright colours, sequins or anything shiny which can be bought in reasonable amounts. I have fabrics that have spider web designs on them, and stars and butterflies. When shopping, I will usually buy a fabric because it is visually intriguing or interesting to touch and then work out how to include it in a story later. I have boxes and boxes of fabrics that I have collected over the years and that other people have given me.

MASKS

Masks are a common feature of the sessions I run. I use a variety of masks ranging from hand-held Venetian type masks and masks worn on top of the head like a baseball cap to rubber masks that envelop the entire head. I always exercise caution initially because masks can be very alarming for students who are unfamiliar with them. I always introduce the masks slowly and watch carefully for reactions. I will not approach a student who looks alarmed and will withdraw the mask completely if anyone looks as if they are getting upset. I usually start with a bird or an animal mask – a domesticated animal like a dog or a cat rather than a lion or a wild animal. The most natural reaction for a student when putting on the mask of a wild animal is to 'act' wild so I usually introduce the wild animal masks gradually.

I let students see the mask before I put it on and I teach them a ritual of how to stop me approaching if they do not like the mask. They learn how to hold up their palm outward and say 'stop' firmly. I then demonstrate with a staff member how this works. I put on the mask and go into role, approach the staff member and have her say 'stop' with the upheld hand. I stop immediately and the students usually laugh and are very keen to have a turn as they sense the power of the firm 'stop'. This exercise is particularly empowering with the scary masks or the fierce animal masks where the students must manage some fear in order to confront and assert themselves.

If you approach a student with the mask on, even if that student has seen you put on the mask and seemed quite happy, if he starts to look unsure or fearful, take off the mask straightaway so that the student can see your familiar face. They often respond with visible signs or relief, or they smile or exhale. They may have forgotten or become very absorbed in the reality of the mask so it is always important to be vigilant. Some students immediately want to try on a mask and you can offer a mirror for them to see themselves. They may then want to interact with other students so you need to remind them that they have to stop when told. Some students may just want to feel and smell the mask. As always, it is the students' own choice and we never coerce the student to go further with the mask than they are comfortable.

With new students or those who have not worked with me for a while, I am especially vigilant with the masks. I usually begin by showing the mask to the students and describing who it is or asking them what it is. I ask them to make the animal sound that goes with the mask. I make sure I do not approach with the mask unless to hold it limply and show that it is simply rubber and nylon or whatever. Then I ask them, 'Shall I put it on?'

Some students are fascinated by masks and will gaze at a face in a mask more intently than at a naked face. Some autistic students display a lot of curiosity about my face in a mask. Nervous students can be supported by having a member of staff sit beside them or even have their chair pulled back so that they are seated further away. Most students learn to tolerate and then enjoy looking at the mask and watch or interact with someone wearing it, although I don't *expect* anyone to put it on. Many students are very sensitive about wearing anything on their heads so won't wear a mask. However, there are many who will be keen to try it on.

When I am wearing a mask and approach a student I always watch for the change in his facial expression that indicates that he has forgotten or does not understand it is me in the mask. If I detect a flicker of alarm, I lift the mask and remind him who it is. For five years I worked with Richard who saw me don a multitude of masks and even then I would see that subtle change in expression as I approached him, followed by a huge, slow grin spread across his face as I lifted the mask and he could see my face and hear the familiar voice.

PERCUSSION

Simple percussion that can be used by a range of students can increase both the enjoyment and participation in a story. A rainmaker is a very handy prop and they are easily made. It is a cylindrical tube sealed at both ends. The tube is filled with small rods and beads or beans that flow through the rods making the sound of waves on the shore or rain when the tube is upended.

Props need not be expensive. They can be everyday objects transformed by imagination and a little creative flair. I used cotton wool spray-painted gold to be the golden fleece in the story of Psyche and Amor (see Chapter 10). Choose props according to the students with whom you work. For example, in groups where students explore using their mouths, use props that don't suffer from getting wet and of course check that they are non-toxic and not harbouring any sharp bits.

I always teach students ground rules about the props. I do not allow them to rummage in the props bag at the beginning of the session. I ask students not to snatch props from one another and to treat them with care. Sometimes I will nominate specific students to gather up and replace the props in the bag at the end of the session.

Allocating roles in the story

For many students, listening to a story is a difficult or impossible task due to cognitive, behavioural or communication difficulties. The way that these students can understand the lessons the story has to give is through enacting or watching others enact the story.

There are many opportunities for participation in the story, one of which is to take a role. 'We are not simply listening or reading, but are involved (or can be) with the whole of our being; we are embodying a role or an aspect of the myth' (Watts, 1992, p.46).

Role-play comprises what Peter Slade referred to as personal play. Personal play differs from projected play where children play using objects or an art form like clay or drawing to represent characters in their internal world, in that it is a lot more active. We become imaginative characters and can interact with others and 'in this the whole person is used, in the wider sense' (Slade, 1995, p.3). Both types of play are important at different times, but Slade does stress the importance of action. 'Creativity is an outflow of energy during which interest must manifest itself outside of the self and explode into action' (Slade, 1968, p.68).

In drama therapy, what constitutes role-play is very wide and inclusive: it may be someone who is profoundly disabled wearing a costume and being interacted with 'in role', or a student being able to remember a simple line and deliver it on cue, or a group of students in role as insects all interacting with one another in role. The key element is flexibility. It is our job to find a way to facilitate a student's taking on of a role, whatever his ability. Role-play is involved in playing with the props and doing the tasks, especially if the student can convey some of the emotional tone of the character. Many students have difficulty using their face and posture to convey emotion. They cannot do it on command the way many non-learning-disabled children can. They may be described as 'lacking affect'. However, giving them a context and a series of actions linked to a specific emotion is a very good way to help them practise what they look and feel like. In this way, playing around with role can be very useful.

The key point to remember when allocating roles is the importance of choice. Because the role-play is an opportunity for students to explore metaphorically unconscious as well as conscious issues, it is vital that students choose for themselves what role, if any, they want to play and are never, even subtly, coerced.

Many students with an intellectual disability have had their wishes or needs overridden in the past or adults may have assumed the responsibility of making decisions and choices for them. Offering choice is immensely important if the work is going to be genuinely therapeutic. 'Making choices requires a sense of self; one must tune into one's thinking and feeling functions in order to make a decision. Taking responsibility for one's choice is a learning experience. I can think of no better way for reinforcing a child's selfhood' (Oaklander, 1978, p.230). Unlike life, the choices presented in drama do not have any lasting repercussions or consequences. The student is free to change his mind if the choice does not feel right or results in consequences he wishes to avoid. This respect for the student's choice may demand greater flexibility on the part of the facilitator, but the effect is a fuller and more heartfelt participation from students. There is a useful phrase, 'If you really want people to say "yes" show them they can say "no".' Staff are sometimes bemused as they consider that the student is very good at saying no; however, they may not do it in an appropriate way. A student is free to say no to participating in any part of the session although I will often check with the student if he has changed his mind before I move on. There are situations where I limit choice and this is sometimes in early work with students who are oppositional in behaviour. In some cases, the student interprets greater flexibility from facilitators as an abdication of control and then begins to act as if he is in charge of the session. When this happens, I am more concerned about the student listening and performing tasks as they have been demonstrated, until I can see that he has accepted my leadership and then I can allow more flexibility.

The use of song

As a facilitator, you will experiment with using your voice to achieve a number of goals: to gain attention, to aid comprehension or to express emotion, but nothing quite arrests the attention and focuses groups like the use of a song. Songs must have a simple rhythm and lyrics. Action songs work well as do call and response songs, where you call out a phrase and the group repeats it back. It certainly helps if you use tunes that are already familiar to the group. I began by adapting well-known songs and giving them new lyrics, but I soon discovered that engagement and participation was so enhanced by the use of songs that I began to make up my own. I don't read music and I don't play an instrument (and if you do, you have a huge advantage) but I am very confident in my voice and my ability to carry a tune.

I do not have a good voice, but singing a lot has made my voice stronger. Many people feel self-conscious about singing in public, but students love to hear you sing and a group singing together (or clapping, shaking a shaker or whatever contribution a student can make) is a unique way to feel part of a group.

If you don't feel confident to make up your own songs, enlist the help of a musical friend or colleague. Tell her what you want the song to be about (a tortoise, a journey, a terrible storm) and remind her to keep it simple. Throughout this book, I have provided examples of songs I have devised and written for specific stories. It may strike you, as it has me, that in some cases, the lyrics are truly awful by adult standards but the students love the songs and participate enthusiastically in the singing of them, which is surely the main thing.

Structuring the sessions

Educational researchers point to the importance of structure in work with students who are highly distractible (Douglas, 1980; Keogh and Margolis, 1976; Kopp and Vaughn, 1982; Teeter and Semrud-Clikeman, 1997, all cited in Bortoli and Brown, 2002, p.5). One of the characteristics of students with autism is a desire for a familiar structure and some students can become very distressed if certain features of their environment are not consistent. The existence of an identifiable structure helps them to tolerate and even enjoy the new, unfamiliar elements which are introduced in every session. The amount and frequency of new elements introduced will depend on the personalities of the individuals in the group. It is worth noting that familiarity with the facilitator is also an important factor in the success of the session.

The basic structure of a drama therapy session is warm-up, main event and closure. The warm-up comprises the 'Hello' song where each student is greeted by name and encouraged to respond with a thumbs up or a verbal 'good', and usually an activity which involves the whole group, for example playing with the lycra.

The main event is the enactment of part of the story using props and involving tasks practised in the warm-up. The story is told in small bite-sized chunks with much repetition, and all activities support and enable participation in the activity that follows which is usually of greater challenge or difficulty.

The stabilizer is the removal of all costumes and stowing of props in the bag and the students return to their seats. I often take the opportunity to reiterate the story thus far and ask questions to ascertain comprehension where appropriate. With some groups, I will tell them the questions I will ask at the beginning of the following session. For example, I might say, 'Who went down to the river to wash her clothes?' When they answer, 'The old lady,' I tell them to remember that for the following week. We finish by singing the 'Goodbye' song.

The telling of stories

It is only in certain contexts that I narrate a story from beginning to end. The level of concentration and verbal acuity needed for such an exercise to be meaningful is usually beyond the reach of most of the students with whom I work. Instead, I organize the story into small pieces that are accompanied by action and an opportunity for the students to participate. It is for this reason that you do not need to be a seasoned, confident storyteller who can sustain a complex narrative over a period of time. You just need to know what bit of the story you are concentrating on for that particular session and link it back to what has gone before. With some groups, I do not even look for any understanding of the content of the story, but use it purely as a vehicle for providing interactions between students and staff in an enjoyable way.

Visuals can be provided to increase the understanding of the narrative. (For more details, see Chapter 12.) When I am telling the story, I speak slowly, clearly, and for the most part in simple, short sentences. I use my facial expression and the quality of my voice to help clarify meaning. I often introduce the story and describe where it comes from, but realize that for most of the time that is for the benefit of staff rather than students.

In summary, the story needs to have plenty of action and themes with which the students can identify. Ideally, it has sufficient mileage to last for at least three or four sessions, with each session building on the last. The story usually involves a goal, obstacles to the attainment of the goal and people, creatures or personal qualities that support the hero or heroes on their journey to attaining the goal. The student's understanding of the story is enhanced by breaking down parts of the story into 'tasks' which students can perform in front of an audience, in other words, their classmates. Each session includes two or three props that aim to increase the level of student participation and enjoyment of the story.

3

Helping Others

One can see in toddlers and pre-schoolers a strong desire to be of help. In order to do this they need lots of support and teaching (and time and space to spill things and make a mess) but we provide this support because we understand that the desire is part of children wanting to take their place in the world and play their part even at such a young age. Helping others builds a sense of belonging and self-worth in children. It also lets them learn in a very real way. In contrast, disabled students are often the passive recipients of help and support and never the providers. This absence emphasizes how marginalized they are, while denying them opportunities for personal growth.

All four stories in this chapter deal with social behaviour in various forms. The first two give examples of characters that express a natural human desire to try to alleviate another's suffering and show very swiftly how the tables turn. The message is 'Help others: you never know when you may need help.' Rata goes into the forest to take what he feels he needs. The myriad little bugs and birds help the tree. Later, when Rata shows some consideration, they also gladly help him to create a wonderful boat. The message is 'You do not have to grab without awareness of others. If you ask, you have no idea how generous the world can be.' In the Tibetan story of the umbrella tree, a character gives to others without any expectation or need of anything in return. He is the truly altruistic character. All four stories share an underlying message of actions having consequences – what goes around, comes around. The concept of actions having consequences, both for others and ourselves, is a difficult concept for many young people to understand, not just those with an intellectual disability. In enacting the stories, we can increase and deepen their understanding of these important issues.

The children and the thunder god

An old man and two children are working in the fields on a very hot day. Suddenly it begins to rain and the sound of thunder can be heard rumbling in the distance. The old man orders the children into the house, gets down a chicken cage, which he sets on the porch, picks up a huge chopper, and stands waiting. Suddenly, there is a great crack of lightning and a crash of thunder and down from the heavens descends the thunder god whom the old man chases with the chopper. He manages to trap the god in the chicken cage and abruptly the rain and thunder stop. He tells the children that under no account are they to give the god any water and that he is off to the village to get herbs and salt to pickle the thunder god.

As soon as he goes, the god begins to plead with the children for water. They are tenderhearted children and feel sorry for him. Carefully, they approach the cage and stroke a drop of water onto his fingertips. Instantly, he recovers his strength and breaks free of the cage. The rain begins to fall in earnest and the storm rages. In gratitude for their help, the thunder god gives the children a seed and tells them to plant it quickly if they want to live. He then ascends to heaven as the floodwaters rise.

Hurriedly, the children plant their seed and watch as it miraculously grows into a vine and then an enormous gourd before their very eyes. They cling to their gourd and float off on the flood. Meanwhile, the old man has found himself a boat and he sails off to the Lord of Heaven to plead for his intercession.

'Please,' he says, 'please, stop the flood.'

The Lord of Heaven listens to the man and orders the thunder god to curb the storm. The thunder god does this so suddenly that the floodwaters subside too rapidly. The old man's boat capsizes and he drowns. The children, however, sail to safety and find themselves the sole survivors of the deluge.

When they grow up the boy suggests that they marry. The girl is initially reluctant but says she will if he can beat her in a race. He does, they marry and become the parents of the future generations.

Themes in the story

The elemental themes in what is essentially a Chinese deluge myth provide numerous dramatic possibilities. It has at its heart the image of the two children responding with kindness to the plight of the thunder god and it is this act of mercy that saves their lives. The images in the story are very vivid: the old man with the chopper saying, 'Get in the house,' the thunder god in the chicken cage, the king of heaven. I try to use masks and fabrics with the classical Chinese colours of red and gold that are very appealing to students and easy to see.

Ideas for the story

SETTING THE SCENE – THUNDER

There is a song often sung in playschool and kindergarten: 'I hear thunder, I hear thunder, Hark, don't you, hark, don't you, Pitter patter rain drops, pitter patter rain drops, I'm wet through, so are you!' It is sung to the tune of 'Frère Jacques' and simple enough for students to become familiar with it over two or three sessions if they don't already know it. I began every session after the 'Hello' song with a long length of sky blue material covered in polka dots that I extended, with me holding one end and a staff member the other. We sang the song, wafting the fabric up and down, and at 'so are you!' pointed to two students to come and sit under the 'rain' and another two, and another two until the whole class was seated under the wafting fabric. As with all the activities, you need to be sensitive to age appropriateness, but I was amazed at how much even older students enjoyed reaching up their hands to touch the fabric.

THE USE OF PERCUSSION

The creation of the storm using percussion is an exercise full of learning potential. I use a range of small drums, shakers and a pair of cymbals. Some students may need support to hold the instruments although you can get shakers that can be velcroed to a wrist. In some groups, you may just want to create as much banging and crashing noises as possible. However, depending on the group, you may be able to orchestrate a storm by dividing students up into 'rain' (shakers or little drumming sounds), 'storm' (drums and anything that makes a loud noise) and 'thunder' (hitting a cymbal) and teach them to watch you for their cue when to come in. When we have convincingly recreated the sound of a storm I ask students to place their instruments under their chairs while we proceed with the next part of the story.

There is a scene involving the old man and the thunder god that is often very popular with students. I portray the character as a very grumpy old man (we know he drowns later in the story so I don't want to elicit too much sympathy for him). He is working in the fields when it begins to rain. I hold out my hand and sign rain. This is the cue for the 'rain' people to begin playing. I then gesture with a thumb and say very gruffly, 'Get in the house.' This is the cue for the 'storm' to begin. I go to the props bag and get a toy chopper. I come back to centre stage, put a hand behind my ear and say, 'I hear thunder.' This is the cue for the cymbals and for the person playing the thunder god to come down from the sky and for me to chase him round the back of the semi-circle until I trap him in a chicken cage.

The thunder god costume is a piece of red fabric and a Chinese mask. This costume is very striking and attractive to students and the mixture of black and red make it very easy to see. The stylized expression on the mask is intriguing to many of the students. If you do not have a chicken cage or similar (any cage big enough for most students to squeeze into) I would simply use the device of getting the students to curl up small and cover with a piece of lycra.

The cessation of the storm at this point makes the scene very dramatic and you can rehearse it so that those playing instruments watch the action so that they stop when they see the thunder god curl into a ball. Not every class will be able to do this, as it requires quite a high level of skill and the ability to divide attention and do two things at the same time. Students have to play their instrument, watch and remember to stop at the right time. Nevertheless, for those who can it is a wonderful exercise. In profoundly disabled groups, staff may be responsible for providing many of the sound effects but the students can experience the theatrical intensity.

As discussed earlier, any story can be adapted to suit the mixed abilities of the students involved. Several of the stories I use involve one character being chased very noisily by another character and it is something that students really enjoy both watching and participating in. It is straightfor-ward enough for students in wheelchairs to be chased as long as support staff assist. Students who move with difficulty or very slowly can also be supported, with the 'old man' chasing in slow motion. It is very important for all students to be as active as they can. This can be a challenge with students with multiple disabilities or older students who are reluctant for various reasons to exert themselves. However, if the physical task is part of the fabric of the story and involves plenty of fun and encouragement, students are much more likely to want to participate.

LABAN BODY SHAPES

There is a section in this story that gives a perfect opportunity to explore Laban's four body shapes (Laban, 1980). The four body shapes are the wall, the ball, the pin and the twist. They provide a very simple model, which we can use to extend students' physical experience.

1. The **wall** shape is where we extend our bodies out as much as we can widthways. We make our legs and arms as wide as we can.

2. The **ball** shape involves making ourselves as small as we can with legs and arms tucked in and head down.

3. The **pin** shape is created when we stretch up with our arms as high as we can and make ourselves as narrow as possible. We stand on tiptoes to make ourselves as tall as we can.

4. The **twist** involves turning from the mid section, twisting the top half of the body.

In the story, the thunder god is trapped inside the cage by the old man. He has to curl up small and maintain that posture while pleading with the children for water. Once he has regained his strength, he bursts out of the cage and becomes big and powerful. You can practise with the students this movement from curled up, confined shape to wide, expanded shape.

Every posture we assume with our bodies activates a corresponding emotion and how we respond to a particular posture is entirely personal. Thus, one child might feel trapped by the ball shape while another may feel secure. One child might feel powerful as the wall while another may feel exposed. Moreover, these responses may change from day to day or moment to moment. The model gives ways to play around with different shapes and it involves the students in an exploration of different levels.

According to Laban, there are three levels, high, medium and deep. The pin commonly involves the high level although you could make a pin shape along the floor. The ball shape is commonly on the deep level and the twist is at medium level.

Later in the story, there is an opportunity to explore all four shapes in a sequence. The thunder god gives the children the seed to plant. We all become the seed, which is small and curled up (ball), and then a shoot begins to grow out of the seed up toward the sun (pin). That shoot becomes a vine that snakes along the floor (twist) and from the vine grows a big, fat, pumpkin (wall).

I noticed that often the students extended their arms to make a wall but forgot about their legs and feet and had to be encouraged to widen their stance. Some students were reluctant to extend their arms possibly because it can feel an exposing posture and it alters the breathing (it opens the chest). Nevertheless, when the shapes are encapsulated in the story the child is absorbed in the activity and extends himself physically in a way he wouldn't do normally. He is focused on creating an image with his body rather than the successful achievement of a physical task.

PLANTING THE SEEDS
This is a wonderfully grounding activity for students and is very attractive for those operating primarily on the sensory level. I like it because the seed is also a positive image of what children are – something full of potential that just needs the right conditions, a bit of care and attention in order to grow and bear fruit. I fill an old cat litter tray with clean sand from the builder's yard. For the seed, I give them sweet chestnuts because they are big, shiny and non-toxic. (In the original story, the god pulls out a tooth and tells them to plant it in the ground.) Each child takes a turn to plant their 'seed' and cover it with sand without uncovering any of the others. Some children may need hand-over-hand assistance with plenty of time to feel the sand trickling through their fingertips. Some children may be able to watch, take note and remember where the previous 'seeds' have been planted.

In one class where I had had a range of needs, most of the students were in wheelchairs and had multiple disabilities while there was one student, Jared, who was very autistic and used to observe the session from under the safety of a crash mat at the back of the classroom. While we played with the sand with the other students, he demonstrated great interest by getting out from under his mat and running over to us and then retreating to his mat. He did this a number of times but could not be enticed to stay longer. At the end of the session, I asked the teacher if I could leave the tray on a table where he could explore it if he wished. We did this and Jared came over and began to flick the sand out of the tray onto the table. Staff then removed the tray. As Jared was a student who was very difficult to engage in anything and highly restless and distractible, I asked staff if they could put out the tray again and not worry about the mess. A dustpan and brush could take care of any mess and I was curious to see what Jared would do.

The tray remained on the table all week and staff reported that Jared continued to flick sand and then seemed to lose interest. However, in the session when we again 'planted the seeds', Jared joined us momentarily. He placed both hands in the tray while facing away. He wriggled his fingers and made happy vocal sounds. He began to return to his crash mat but an astute staff member placed a chair slightly nearer the circle and encouraged Jared to sit down. He did so and this became his place for the sessions, except those days when he was distressed or feeling insecure.

The bell of Hamana

A woodcutter from the village of Hamana goes into the forest to chop down trees. He comes upon a clearing where he finds a huge old tortoise lying upside down on its shell. The tortoise cannot move. It is stuck. It will die if someone does not help it. The wood-cutter uses all his strength to push the tortoise back up the right way. The tortoise thanks the woodcutter and disappears into the forest.

The woodcutter continues through the forest until he finds a great tree to cut down. He takes up his axe. On the first strike, a great roar goes out in the forest. The woodcutter stops what he is doing and listens. He chops the tree again and the roars come again, nearer this time. He stops and peers into the blackness of the under-growth. He is afraid and does not know what to expect. Suddenly, out from the forest come fierce forest animals – the lion, the tiger, and the wolf. They are snarling and angry with the man for cutting down the trees. They tell him they are going to kill him and tear him to pieces. They continue to advance towards him padding on their huge paws. The woodcutter thinks his end has come. He drops down on his knees and begins to plead with the animals.

Suddenly a loud voice shouts, 'Stop!' Everything in the forest stops. Everything is still. There is no noise, no birdsong or the repetitive sound of cicadas. Then out from the trees comes the tortoise, the great, old tortoise whom the woodcutter saved. He speaks in a calm voice to the angry beasts, 'This man is my friend. Do not harm him.'

The animals are still angry. They want to kill the man. 'Look what he is doing to the forest. Soon there will be no more trees,' says the lion.

The tortoise speaks again, 'This man is my friend. He helped me.'

Finally, the animals listen and they slink away, growling and resentful. The man is very grateful to the tortoise. He says, 'You saved my life.'

The tortoise says, 'Just as you saved mine.'

The tortoise gives the man a gift – a great bell to take back to his village. It is the first bell of the Mandingo civilization.

'Every time you sound the bell,' the tortoise says, 'remember that you share the forest with the animals – and have a responsibility to maintain it not just for yourself but for every creature that lives there.'

The man promises and returns to Hamana with the special gift.

Themes in the story

In common with many of the stories, there is an ecological message about caring for the environment and others who share it with us. There is the familiar theme of one good deed deserves another. The woodcutter appears to lack awareness of the impact his actions have on other living things and this ignorance almost brings about his undoing. The intercession of the tortoise, who despite age and being physically unprepossessing, appears to command respect amongst the other creatures in the forest, saves the woodcutter. His task is then to take the message back to others in his village and the bell is a fitting symbol of that message which is as clear as a bell.

Ideas for the story
FIERCE FOREST ANIMALS

Animals appear in many of the stories and are very popular with most of the students. It is generally easier for them to convey the essence of an animal than to role-play a person. Masks are a visual, tactile and interactive way to help students understand what the animal is, and the role it plays in the story. I have many animal masks ranging from simple foam rubber hats that have the animal on top, to plastic masks, to full-face and head rubber masks with nylon hair. I also have a variety of hand puppets that I will occasionally use with any student who looks alarmed by the masks. See the previous chapter for more detailed information on how to use masks.

The 'fierce forest animal' masks are useful at providing the challenge the student has to overcome. Challenge is an important component in the sessions. Some students are not very good at saying or demonstrating when they don't like something. They may signal no by refusing to engage in what is offered or by reacting catastrophically. I use these masks to teach the power of the firm, clear 'no'. I demonstrate a routine for confronting and keeping the 'fierce forest animal' at bay. I show students how to hold up the flat of their hands close to their body. They do not need to extend their arms. They accompany the gesture with a firm 'stop.' Nonverbal students simply make the gesture as forcefully as they can. I then demonstrate the routine with a staff member. I approach her threateningly in the mask and she firmly and calmly holds up her hand and says, 'Stop.' I react by immediately backing off. Some students begin to laugh at this stage either because they are relieved or because they see the possibilities in such power. I then ask, 'Who would like a turn?' Usually the bravest is very keen to have his turn and, of course, no one has to have a turn who doesn't want one. By the end, I am going around the semi-circle trying to intimidate but being calmly kept at bay by each student in turn. This is a useful exercise for teaching cause and effect and empowering students with a sense of their right to defend their boundaries in an appropriate manner.

THE TORTOISE AND PROPRIOCEPTION

Proprioception is the word used to describe body awareness. It is the sense involved in making continual, automatic adjustments in our position. Problems with proprioception mean the student has to think about basic functions that should be automatic. This can affect his ability to pay attention to other things happening in his environment which, consequently, has a negative impact on his learning. Students can be unsteady on their feet and fear falling over as their spatial awareness is affected. Problems with proprioception are common in students with an intellectual disability. The proprioceptive sense is stimulated by push/pull activities, weight-bearing activities and deep pressure or firm touch (Mailloux, 1993).

It seemed to me that the tortoise with his heavy shell could provide a wonderful opportunity to help activate the proprioceptive sense in students.

Initially, with the smaller students, I used myself as the tortoise, getting down on my hands and knees and getting the student to lie over my back. I would then plod slowly along balancing the student on my back. If you think this is dedication beyond the call of duty, remember that this was in the early days of my working with students, when I was scrabbling around trying to find activities which they enjoyed, and anything that created a bond between us was an advantage. Although I don't tend to role-play the tortoise any more, I am very physical in sessions. I do chase students, play-fight with them and fall out of boats with them. It is for this reason that I limit myself to a maximum of four sessions a day. If you are the teacher of a class wanting to work in this way, you would probably only want to do sessions like this once a week. The upside is the clear enjoyment of the students who are getting to experience an adult in a completely different way. Many students in special schools have not had the play opportunities, or the rough and tumble of a normal childhood. In drama, I want to provide some of those experiences.

I developed the idea of the weight-bearing tortoise that must always carry his home on his back from the sand-filled bags that are used to support students with profound physical disabilities and sometimes to still a fidgety, hyperactive student. I used a green cushion cover filled with sandbags and draped it over the student's back. It had to be heavy enough to slow movement but not so heavy that the student could not move. It made it clear how impossible the tortoise would have found it to turn over of his own accord without the woodcutter's assistance. It also made it much more of a physical struggle for the woodcutter as 'he' was having to push another student plus heavy sandbags.

When I've played the tortoise and asked students for help there are usually several who respond straightaway and who immediately begin pulling and pushing me in all different directions. With a few suggestions from support staff, they will work together to all push and pull in the right direction to upend the tortoise. In this way, the story provides yet another opportunity for students to work together to accomplish a goal.

THE BELLS

Although the story describes one great bell, I usually bring in a variety of chimes, a xylophone and assorted little bells for the students to play. Together we sing the bell song to the tune of 'Speed, bonny boat'.

Ring out the bell
Ring it high, ring it low
Filling the air with sound
Remember the tortoise
For then you'll know
What goes around, comes around.

Rata the wanderer

Rata went into the forest to find wood to make a waka (canoe) to search for the bones of his father. In the middle of the forest, he found a beautiful tree. Taking his axe, he chopped down the tree. He worked hard and it took him most of the day. He trimmed the branches and left it ready to carve the next day. He took careful note of the tree's location. Then he set off home for his dinner.

As soon as he left, all the little creatures of the forest came out, the birds, the bugs and the butterflies. Together they lifted the tree, put it back in its place and replaced all the branches. They even replaced all the tiny woodchips around the trunk.

Next day Rata returned to carve the wood and was amazed to find the tree standing in its place. He knew it was the same tree because there was the imprint the trunk had made as it laid in the grass. He was very confused and a little frightened but he took up his axe and chopped the tree down again. Again, he trimmed the branches and left it ready to carve the following day. He looked around the forest before he left but he could see nothing amiss. He set off home to have his dinner. As soon as Rata left, all the little creatures came. They worked together to put the tree back up. They replaced the branches and the little woodchips at its base.

When Rata returned the next day and saw the tree standing as before, he was amazed and annoyed. He could not understand what was happening. He set to and chopped down the tree a third time. It took him all day. However, when he left, instead of going home, he hid behind a tree to see what would happen. Within a few minutes, all the little birds and insects came out and started to restore the tree. Rata could not believe his eyes. He rushed out from behind the tree shouting, 'Stop! That is my tree!'

However, all the little birds and insects said to Rata, 'Who gave you leave to take this tree?'

Rata was dumbfounded. It had not occurred to him to ask before he took the tree. 'What nonsense is this? The tree belongs to me. I chose it out of all the trees of the forest.'

The little creatures replied, 'It is not your tree. To take anything from the forest you must ask permission of Tane, the god of the forest.'

Rata was ashamed and sorry. He said, 'What shall I do? I need to make a waka to go and find the bones of my father.'

The little birds and insects said to Rata, 'If you ask respectfully, you will be given.'

Rata called out in a loud voice, 'Please may I have this tree so that I can make a waka to search for the bones of my father?'

Suddenly, Tane, the god of the forest appeared. He was smiling. He said, 'Take the tree with my blessing.'

The forest creatures said, 'We will help you make your waka, Rata.'

Once the tree was felled, the insects and the birds with their tiny beaks carved the most wonderful designs all over the waka, making it the finest you would ever see. Rata was overjoyed. He thanked the forest and sailed off across the ocean.

Themes in the story

A strong message in the story is of the importance of asking permission before assuming you can take something. This is a useful message to reiterate in the school environment, but it obviously has wider implications to do with the impact on the environment of man not being aware of his responsibilities as well as his rights. It is a clear illustration of how powerful a group can be when they work together even if individual members are small. The little bugs and birds are able to restore the huge tree and bring about a complete change in Rata's attitude.

Ideas for the story

Rata is one story that gives a wonderful opportunity to see how much of a culture of gentleness and care for one another you have managed to create with the group. A major task in the story is chopping down the tree. For the chopping, I use a plastic axe. The tube of green jersey material, so useful for crawling through, now serves as a costume for the person who is playing the tree.

Whenever I demonstrate for the students how I want them to do the task, I get raised eyebrows from staff who are unfamiliar with this way of working. Their expectation is clearly that once the student has possession of the axe he will wreak havoc or at least use it to hit the person playing the tree. I have done this story many, many times and I have never seen a child take the opportunity that the role affords of deliberately hurting either myself or the staff member playing the tree. I think this demonstrates that students are not innately aggressive and in a group where they feel safe and secure there is no reason why they should deliberately hurt anyone else.

I am always very careful to break the task down and be very explicit about the three stages and we prepare by practising on a cardboard box first so I can see the student's level of physical ability in wielding the axe. The only time I have been struck was when the student lacked the ability to control the axe or estimate correctly the distance between the swing and the 'tree'. Students practise holding the axe correctly with both hands and I then place the cardboard box in front of them and they have to hit it three times. If they successfully complete this task, they are ready to chop down the 'tree'.

When choosing a staff member to play the tree I will often choose someone who I know is well liked by the students. I instruct the staff member to make sounds to accompany the chopping so that the student can experience some satisfaction that his actions are having an effect without him actually having to hit the tree. The louder the 'ouch' from the 'tree' the more the students giggle. I break the task down into three actions.

1. Take the axe in both hands (the student will have more control using both hands).

2. Raise the axe above your head with a big intake of breath (this makes it look as if the axe is heavy rather than a plastic toy).

3. Bring it down with a loud 'chop' but stop just short of the staff member's leg.

It is amazing how often students can achieve this task considering it is so complex and involves a lot of hand–eye coordination. If students need support, I give it but am careful to let them have a chance to do it on their own first. I try not to step in too quickly. I trust them to get it right. It is amazing how often children sense our expectations and respond accordingly. They will meet our expectations if we expect them to be careful and trustworthy just as much as if we expect them to take advantage of the situation in order to hurt someone. Usually it takes about three or four chops for the tree to fall. If the staff member can do it gradually that is best as it gives a real sense of anticipation and achievement, but it is more difficult for the staff member. There is great excitement when the tree is felled and 'Rata' can go round and chop off a few branches too to make a fine piece of wood all ready for carving.

MAKING THE WAKA

The staff member who played the 'tree' sits up to become the figurehead of the waka and the students fall in behind her sitting on the ground with their legs straddling each other. Depending on ability, the waka can move by everyone shuffling on their bottoms. With some classes it is possible to 'paddle' the waka by having a staff member in front demonstrating right and left and the students have to lean in that direction at the same time. It is also a good time to sing a rowing song or anything with a faintly nautical theme. It takes great care to get out of the waka without capsizing. The student on the end of the line is the first to get up and so on up to the last person, the figurehead.

ROLE-PLAYING THE TINY CREATURES

I use a combination of bird masks, butterfly and ladybird wings and bumblebee hand puppets. I bring each item out one at a time and ask students to identify what it is and if any sound goes with it. Everybody has a turn and I often ask students which was their favourite. When it comes to the appearance of the little creatures in the story, I make the props available and students come and put on their costume. Together they help the tree and I might encourage them to fly around a little in order to sustain the role for longer and give them opportunities to interact with one another in role. The advantage of these creatures is that they are mostly gentle and non-combative and so they interact with one another on that basis. It would be tricky to have the fierce forest animals interact as freely, as inevitably they would end up trying to eat each other. Although some students may be unable to answer questions or signal choices, with sensitivity and creativity, they can be assisted to participate and have fun trying on costumes and masks.

THE SONGS

A piece of moss-coloured fabric provides an ideal forest canopy to waft over students' heads as we sing the forest song adapted from the tune of 'On top of old Smokey'. The names of the creatures mentioned in the song were suggested by a group of 8-year-olds from a discussion about the animals of the New Zealand forest or bush.

> Here in the forest
> All lovely and green
> I see all the creatures
> That rarely are seen.
> The ant and the morepork
> The fantail and bee
> The lizard and kiwi
> All live in our tree.
> The spider, kereru
> The butterfly too
> The ladybird, magpie
> Are calling to you.

The morepork is a type of owl, the fantail is a little bird and kereru is Maori for woodpidgeon. You may want to substitute other more easily recognizable creatures for your client group depending on the part of the world in which you live.

The chopping song

> Here is a tree
> It's a very nice tree
> Going to pick up my axe and chop
> Going to chop in the middle
> Going to chop in the bottom
> Going to chop in the top, top, top.
> Chop, chop, chop, do you see it falling?
> Chop, chop, chop, let there be no stalling

Chop, chop, chop, can you hear me calling?
Timber, Timber.

In one class, a student who was usually very reserved and scarcely made a sound began to call out 'timber' on cue. Students love doing the chopping movements to accompany the song. One teacher drew a tree on a huge piece of paper and the students covered it with pictures of birds, lizards and insects that they had drawn, coloured in or cut out of magazines. Their experience of the story was enriched by this creative use of a number of different media. For a detailed description of a session using this story, see Chapter 13.

The umbrella tree

A young man called Palden is travelling throughout Tibet when he stops for a rest in a beautiful forest. He chooses a huge, old umbrella tree to snooze under and settles down on the mossy part around the roots under the shelter of the shady branches. He only means to sleep a short while, but he must have been more tired than he thought, for when he awakes darkness has fallen and looking out into the gloom of the forest he sees hundreds of yellow eyes glowing in the darkness. He realizes that what woke him up were the sounds of wild animals approaching and the cracking of twigs and undergrowth as they came nearer and nearer. He is very afraid, so he quickly shins up the tree and shelters in the branches where he has a good view of the forest floor below.

What he sees and hears amazes him, for as he watches, a snow lion, wolves, foxes, bears and all manner of wild beasts make a circle underneath the umbrella tree and begin to speak. The snow lion appears to be the leader. The beasts discuss all manner of things, but chiefly the ways in which man destroys the forest with his lack of wisdom and is so often the agent of his own unhappiness.

'Yes,' says the monkey, 'I have a story from the village over the way there; you know the one where the headman has the sick child?'

Some of the other animals nod.

'They have tried everything to cure the girl, but to no avail, and she is very near death. In front of the house is a huge rock and under it is a sick frog suffering from lack of water. If they gave that frog water, they would see their child improve. However, they just don't think like that do they?'

'No, no,' agreed many of the other animals. 'And they wouldn't listen to us either, would they?' Soon after, a growing light heralded the coming dawn and each of the beasts slunk, slid, or flew off into the forest.

When all is quiet again, Palden eases himself down from the tree and brushes himself down. He is stiff and sore, but very excited and he cannot wait to make his way to the village described by the monkey and find the house of the headman. When he gets there all is hushed and subdued. There is an air of great sadness over the house and Palden is afraid that he is too late to save the girl. However, he knocks on the door and asks the woman who answers about the sick girl.

The woman shakes her head and says, 'We have tried everything but she will not rally. Her father is heartbroken.'

Palden asks if there is any objection to him trying something and the woman says, 'No, but we have tried everything.'

He asks if he can look at the rock in front of the house and sure enough, he finds a tiny shrivelled frog with parched skin and cloudy eyes, just as the monkey described. He asks for water and the frog revives. Its eyes become bright and its skin green and lustrous. Accompanied now by curious family members he asks to see the young girl. As they approach the house, they hear the sound of voices raised in excitement, and coming into the bedroom they find the child sitting up asking for food and with colour in her cheeks.

The headman turns to Palden bursting with gratitude and says, 'What can I give you? Name anything and it is yours'.

Palden shakes his head and says, 'I don't want anything. It is enough for me to see your daughter well.'

The villagers persuade Palden to stay for a feast in his honour and give him many gifts.

Soon he is on his way again, back to the forest and that selfsame tree. He gets there just as dusk is falling and makes himself comfortable in the branches and waits. Sure enough, under the blanket of the night the wild beasts come. Once more, they convene a meeting and begin to talk of many things, but once again, the topic turns to the madness of men. It is the bear this time who says, 'You know that village on the far side of the forest? They scrabble every day for water – coming all the way into the valley to fetch water from the river because they think there is none in the village. If only they dug under the roots of that old tree in the village square, there is a mountain stream with fresh water for everyone right under their noses.'

The animals all shake their heads in amazement at the ignorance of man and turn to other matters. Eventually, just before dawn they disperse and slink off into the forest.

Palden slides down from his perch and begins to journey across the mountain until he comes to the village the bear had described. He is hot and tired when he gets there and stops at a house to ask for a cup of water. The woman whose house it is says, 'You are welcome to a drink but we have little to give you. We have to travel every day to find water and it is much work and labour.'

Palden says to her, 'What would you say if I told you there was water here in the village to which you could help yourself when you felt like it: good, fresh water from the mountain?'

'I would be amazed,' says she 'and more grateful than I could say. But what water are you talking about?'

Palden points to the huge old tree stump that is right in the centre of the village. He says, 'We need help to pull it up and people to dig.'

The young man's authority is such that the villagers quickly comply and harness eight yaks to pull up the stump, while others jump down in the hole and begin to dig. For a while, there is nothing but the sound of men working, then suddenly the hole begins to pool with water, fresh and clean. The villagers quickly fill their pots and gourds and drink deeply. They are overjoyed and beg Palden to name his price, but again he is reluctant to take anything. One man suggests he settle in the village and they will build him his own little house. Eventually Palden agrees and he ends up marrying and living very happily in the village.

Themes in the story

The theme of the interrelationship between people and everything else that lives is stated explicitly in this story. The fate of the headman's daughter is intimately bound with that of the little green frog. The power of altruism is another theme. The story demonstrates that there is an appropriate attitude towards information and that it is to be used for the good of all. It is definitely not exploitative. The hero in the story does not seek his own self-advancement but is driven by a desire to help others, and that brings its own reward.

With groups, I usually finish the story at the point where Palden settles down to live happily ever after but the original ending of the story is interesting to note. In the complete version, an old friend who is curious to know how Palden has come across such good fortune visits him. Palden tells him about the animals and how to find the tree in the forest. The friend immediately sees the potential in such knowledge and makes his way to the tree planning to make himself a rich man. Unfortunately, the branch he is lying on breaks and deposits him right in the middle of the circle of wild beasts who waste no time killing and eating him! Palden is not greedy; he does not keep going back to the umbrella tree.

The theme of greed and how insatiability proves one's undoing is a common one in stories. Once Palden has his basic needs met, he settles down to enjoy his life. This aligns the story with others with an environmental theme describing a balance in nature, which animals are aware of but people are not. This theme is mirrored in 'The bell of Hamana', 'Rata' and many other stories. It is an important theme for children generally because it is teaching them about the importance of care. They must learn to care for themselves, each other and their environment. Of course, the most effective way we have of teaching our students to care is to model caring in all our encounters with them.

Ideas for the story

Journeys are a common feature of many of the stories in this book and are often an opportunity to provide a physical challenge for students. With the assistance of staff, it is relatively simple to transform classrooms into arduous terrain with chairs to walk over, rope to balance on and tables to crawl under. I always first check with the teacher, that what I am going to ask students to do does not undermine any classroom rules, such as not to climb on tables. It is possible to bring in props to provide the challenges, like blue lengths of cloth to be rivers to jump over, cushions to be stepping stones, and the tube can always be used to crawl through. For students who need more concrete experiences I have provided real rocks, trays of sand, slippery seaweed or, on one memorable occasion, armfuls of a flowering bush that had to be pushed through. Journeys work well across a range of abilities. Students in wheel-chairs or walking frames can still embark on the journey even if it only comprises being wheeled out of the classroom along the corridor and back into the classroom through another door.

In psychological terms, the journey represents a movement from one place to another and, like any transition, is potentially fraught with danger.

CLIMBING THE TREE

I have on occasions taken the class outside to climb on the jungle gym, but more often I have used a rope. For this, it is necessary to have a room with a beam strong enough to take a student's weight. The rope is common-or-garden thick rope. I tie a big knot in the end, then sling the knot over the beam, and catch it the other side. The process of slinging the knot is all part of the session so it doesn't matter if it takes a few tries as you will be virtually guaranteed everyone's undivided attention. Sometimes I tie a red cloth to the end of the rope so it is easier to see.

If students are physically able to climb rope this is their chance to shine. A strong staff member holds onto the other end to provide ballast and the child can climb up. One student who was very hyperactive shinned up the rope and climbed along the beam in a matter of seconds. The height was only about 2 metres and I stood below him ready to catch him but he was very physically agile and thankfully responded immediately when we calmly asked him to 'come down and let someone else have a turn'.

Many students are unable to shin up the rope so we ask them to sit on the knot of the rope and use it like a swing. Or they can sit while we pull the rope up and another staff member can support them to reach up and touch the beam. With some students, the experience of climbing the rope will be having it held above them while they stretch up and place hand over hand. For some students who are very physically disabled it may consist of having the rope drawn very gently along their open palm. When there is no beam to throw the rope over, I line it up on the floor and the challenge is to walk along it without falling off. The best way to do this is barefoot. This is called the horizontal climb and it increases sensitivity to the feet, improves balance and concentration.

You know your environment, your students and what they are capable of, so adapt the exercise accordingly. Think creatively, and sometimes laterally, about how you could approximate the experience of climbing, if they are physically unable or the environment is not conducive to allowing any risk. Taking risks is a part of growing and learning and many students with a disability are not allowed to do that. I want the special child to have experiences available to the 'normal child' in line with the principles of normalization (Bank-Mikkelson, 1969).

For a story involving a journey up a mountain I bring in a bag of rocks of different shapes and sizes. We can explore various aspects of the rocks, their shape, relative roughness or smoothness, their weight, etc. For students with proprioception problems, we can fill backpacks with rocks and they can carry the bags as we 'climb' up the mountain. We culminate with taking off our shoes and taking a few steps over the rocks. For students in wheelchairs, we can take off their shoes and rub the rocks very gently on the soles of the feet. In one session I saw a student who is often very sleepy jerk back his head and open his eyes really wide when I did this. He maintained this level of alertness for the remainder of the session.

Of course, this approach is consistent with the need to make activities concrete for students with a learning disability. This is a very tangible experience of a mountain and it replicates the experience of a million kids who play barefoot and experience a multitude of different surfaces beneath their feet. Many disabled children never get to do this. They may be protected from many aspects of the environment out of concern for their health.

PUSHING AND PULLING

Pushing and pulling are both activities designed to help with problems of proprioception, increase muscle tone and ground and focus energy. If there is going to be any pushing or pulling in the story I will prepare students in a number of ways. First, I will tell them that we are going to need to be strong and ask them to show me their muscles. Then I will ask them to put up both hands and I will come round and push against their hands to see how strong they are feeling. For students who are very disabled I will be very gentle, but I want them to experience some physical resistance and the tiniest response from them is applauded. With some groups, you can get students to pair up, stand, and push against hands or feet or backs.

Pushing is an important component of what Marian Lindvist, who founded the Sesame method of Movement and Drama, called movement with touch. This technique was designed for work with profoundly disabled individuals and people with autism. She says, 'I'm going to get them feeling that they have *some* strength by offering *some* resistance when I get them to push… They have to come up against resistance – but the resistance must never feel stronger that they are' (Pearson, 1996, p.66). Lindvist uses the word 'will' and describes pushing as a way of invoking a person's will and helping him assert himself. In this way, pushing is the physical correlative of the theme of challenge at the heart of every one of the stories used in this book.

Pulling is a linked activity involving pitting one's strength in a sustained way with the added involvement of grip. With very disabled students who are unable to grip voluntarily some hand-over-hand help can be provided. In order to give the student the experience of exerting himself, the person helping needs to provide sounds of exertion and accompany the movement with the appropriate word. The tree stump in the story provides opportunities to both push and pull. Students can be yaks pulling on ropes or people pushing the tree stump at the same time. Any heavy, cumbersome object will do for the stump. I used a filing cabinet covered with fabric once.

I hope in this chapter to have conveyed some of the many dramatic and therapeutic possibilities when using these stories with groups. As with all the subsequent chapters, it is intended only as a stimulus for your own ideas or a starting point to begin to experiment with this flexible approach.

4

Dealing with Change

Routine appears to be imposed to make life predictable and to impose order, as novelty, chaos or uncertainty are intolerable. It also acts as a means of reducing anxiety... Thus, the establishment of a routine ensures there is no opportunity for change. (Attwood, 1998 p.99)

The resistance to change and desire for predictability and routine so associated with children on the autistic disorder spectrum is common in varying degrees for many of the students in special education. There can also be a tendency to develop fixated, stereotypic behaviours. While the function of this may be to manage anxiety, inevitably these behaviours tend to deny the student access to a wide range of experiences and opportunities.

The consistent structure of the session acknowledges students' need for predictability, while the introduction of some new elements every session provides a realistic challenge. One reason why the drama therapy session is so successful in engaging and retaining attention (see Chapter 13 for an account of research focused on this issue) is that students are not expected to sit still for very long focusing on one particular activity – the activity is always changing.

This group of stories explores metaphorically the desire for everything to stay the same and how impossible a task that is. They convey graphically and surprisingly, the effort required for making changes. While the person with autism may be an extreme example, most people can identify with reluctance to both initiate change and have changes imposed upon them over which they have no control. In the story 'Raven and the giant who sits on the tide', a Kwakiutl story from Canada, we can see how much persistence and patience is required to change long-held beliefs. In the story of Maui and the sun, we witness the effort required to combat passivity and lethargy when Maui has to bully his brothers into accompanying him on his quest. One of the main messages of the North American Indian story of the Windmaker is a warning about trying to appropriate power for which we do not have the responsibility. It is right that there are certain things beyond our control, and power over the elements is one of those things.

Two of the stories describe an interruption to normal daily rhythms. (The story of Maui and the sun, which is a Maori story, describes a 'normal' state that is untenable.) This results in stasis that brings great suffering. It is hard to find a traditional story that does not convey stasis as a negative occurrence – although we struggle with impermanence, it is an unalterable fact of life. Stories often grapple with that most painful of changes about which we have little control – death. In the Gilgamesh epic, the hero endures many hardships to attain the holy watercress of immortality only to lose it to the hungry snake while resting. The English story of death in a nut has Jack tricking death and trapping him in a walnut to stop him taking his mother, only to find that everyone is starving since the animals that provide food are impossible to kill.

These stories describe the necessity for flux and movement, while at the same time acknowledging how difficult it is to live with circumstances outside our control and the inevitability of change.

Raven and the giant who sits on the tide

Raven travels to see his people and finds them all starving. He says to them, 'I filled the ocean full of fish for you. Why are you starving?'

They tell him that the fish have all swam out to the deeper waters and are impossible to catch. Raven asks them what happened to the tides and they tell him they don't know. So Raven goes flying over the ocean. Far out to sea he comes upon a giant sitting muttering to himself, and as he flies close he hears the giant saying over and over, 'I am the giant who sits on the tide. I am the giant who sits on the tide.'

Raven can see this is the culprit so he shouts at the giant, 'Get up, let the tide go!'

But the giant doesn't listen, so Raven flies up high into the sky and then lets himself fall down on the giant who gets such a fright that he leaps to his feet. Having got his attention, Raven sets about teaching the giant how to stand up, sit down, stand up, sit down and change his phrase to, 'I am the giant who moves the tide, stand up, sit down, stand up, sit down.'

Raven flies back to his people and finds the coastline flooded with violent storms and rushing waves. He looks out to sea and can see the grey shape of the giant moving abruptly up and down, so he flies back. He flies in front of the giant and looks him in the eye and then he whispers something in the giant's ear beyond our hearing. The giant shudders and then begins to move more gently, rising slowly at the allotted time and sinking back down into the waves later on. Returning to the villages, Raven finds the people overjoyed at the shallow waters appearing at low tide and the greater ease of catching fish, and he knows that his people need never be hungry again.

Themes in the story

The story contains a common theme of nourishment being abundant but inaccessible to us (see also the Maori story of Kahakura, Chapter 10). On a psychological level, this describes the experience of being surrounded by good things but feeling unable to enjoy them. This can happen when a person's earliest experiences have been characterized by emotional deprivation: the scars from that experience exist into later life. Even when that situation no longer exists on an actual level, it feels as if it does on an inner level.

The giant represents the old pattern that refuses to budge and free up the sustenance that is waiting to flow in. He is a character whose difficulty in adapting to a new role negatively affects the community. Many students have difficulties thinking creatively – once they are taught something, it tends to 'stick'. Many of us were taught information as children which we were not meant to evaluate critically: 'Don't talk to strangers,' 'Keep away from the fire' – very useful information, but some of which we adapted as we grew and sometimes discarded as we became adults. People with an intellectual disability find it difficult to update this kind of information.

The image of the giant is relevant not only to how students may perceive themselves, but also to how others perceive them. Some parents of students with an intellectual disability struggle with their child's growing maturity, particularly in the area of sexuality. Although many students develop at a slower rate to their 'normal' counterparts, they do follow similar patterns and it is for the people around them to make the adaptations appropriate to their age and ability.

Ideas in the story

This story can be explored in many ways but its chief attraction for me was the image of the giant being shouted at to 'stand up' and 'sit down'. When I read the story, it immediately resonated with my experience in special schools where in some classrooms 'stand up' and ' sit down' are two of the most common phrases used. For many students, tasks that are more complex begin with the requirement to stand up, for example, when walking towards someone.

There is also the opportunity for role reversal, in that students playing Raven can shout at the giant (played by a member of the support staff) to stand up and sit down. They experience another perspective: that of having to get someone to do something that they are clearly reluctant to do, and this can be a powerful insight for them.

USE OF THE SWISS BALL

I was working with a class of 6-year-old students who were all quite physically small, and used the tube (see page 33 for a description of the tube) and the Swiss ball (a large inflatable exercise ball). Sitting on the ball, I stretched the tube over both the ball and my legs and pulled it up to my chin. I then asked the class to come and stuff the tube with cushions to make me really fat. Finally, I was this great big ball person with little feet and a head sticking out. The students found this hilarious and loved playing Raven, shouting at me to 'stand up, sit down'. They were all keen to come and be the giant and have the cushions stuffed around them.

CORNFLAKES

Students sit in a circle with one less chair than there are people. The person without a chair stands in the centre of the circle and says, 'Everyone wearing blue, move!' and everyone wearing blue has to change chairs. This is the first person's opportunity to grab a chair and whoever is left standing has to stand in the centre and call out something else to get people moving. If all else fails, the person can call out 'cornflakes' which is the signal for everyone to swap chairs. This game can be more or less sophisticated depending on ability. A variation is to make laminated pictures of fruit and give pairs to people in the group. The person in the centre calls out the name of a fruit and the two people with the fruit have to change chairs. The signal for everyone to move is 'fruit salad!'

Maui and the sun

In the earliest of days, the sun travelled very quickly across the sky. No sooner than people got up they had to go to bed again. It was difficult to accomplish anything in such short days. Maui found it particularly irritating and one evening when he was cooking his meal in the fire, the sun suddenly went down, plunging everything into darkness and Maui ended up burning his supper. He was furious and decided to do something about the sun. He persuaded the rest of the tribe to gather flax and he taught his brothers how to weave the flax into very strong rope that he cut into lengths both short and long. Tying these together, he made a net that was immensely strong.

He bullied his brothers into joining with him and they all embarked on a journey to the land of the sun. They travelled by night so that the sun could not see them approaching and slept during the day, and very soon they found themselves in a parched dry landscape. There they found a huge scorched round hole in the ground, which was where the sun lived. Under Maui's leadership they took clay, made shelters for themselves, and smeared the clay on their bodies. Soon a growing glow signalled that the dawn was coming and that the sun was on his way. 'Quick,' commanded Maui as he threw his magic net over the hole and instructed his brothers to hold on tight. The rising sun found itself trapped by the magic net that did not burn and demanded to know who was there.

'Maui,' said Maui boldly.

'What do you want?' said the sun.

'We want you to slow down,' said Maui.

At this, the sun became outraged that a mere boy could command him, the mighty sun, to do anything and he began to push up against the net with all his might. Maui reminded his brothers to hold on.

Eventually the sun became exhausted and asked again, 'What was it you wanted me to do?'

Maui replied in a loud voice, 'We want you to slow down.'

So the sun agreed to slow down and Maui released him from the net and the sun made a slow ascent into the sky, and until this day it takes much longer for the sun to cross the sky so that we have all the time we need.

Themes in the story

I think it is useful to know the background to this story, the major adaptation I have made, and the reasons for that. Prior to this event, in the traditional Maori myth, Maui tricked his grandmother into giving him her magic jawbone and he uses the jawbone to beat the sun into submission. On first reading this story, I was shocked at the violence done to the sun in order to make it change its course. The story says the sun, beaten so badly by Maui, still shows the scars today as evidenced by the craters on the surface. My immediate interpretation was that the story described man's domination of his environment and I saw it as a stark contrast to the theme of respect for the natural world represented by the story of Rata (see Chapter 3). However, as with all the stories, multiple interpretations are possible. Maui is a trickster character whose actions are sometimes difficult to understand and a challenge to the rational mind. It is one reason I like to include the story of Maui's birth as it gives reasons for why he is so perverse and interested in making mischief (see Chapter 7). The enacting of stories is an important way to gain a unique perspective not always available to the rational mind. In an enactment of the story with adults, a person role-playing Maui described their experience thus:

> I just felt that the sun carried on its own sweet way without regard to how we all were feeling and it made our living conditions oppressive. And it seemed to me that the only way to get its attention was to fight back in the way it would understand and respect. If we went and nicely asked it to change it just wouldn't – we had to force it.

From this perspective, the story describes a revolutionary act. Maui is the leader with the will and the courage to defy the status quo while most of the others can only accept their suffering. In confronting the sun, Maui is challenging an opponent of huge proportions. He exerts his will and beats the sun into submission and a profound change is brought about. I wanted to retain the vigour and resourcefulness of Maui but modify the violence of the beating of the sun with the jawbone and make it appropriate for use in an educational setting. Therefore, as soon as we trapped the sun in the magic net and we had his attention, we raised and extended our index fingers and pointing them at the sun chanted forcefully 'slow down'. The gesture is a great diminution, but nevertheless it can still carry power, as most of the students know that you are not supposed to point your finger at anyone, and so it carries a frisson of presumptuousness. Students really enjoy wagging their finger at the sun and hearing him get angry under the net but knowing that he is unable to do anything about it until he does what he is told.

MAKING THE NET

Here in New Zealand, we are lucky enough to have flax readily available but if you don't have flax or an equivalent, rope will do just as well. Give everyone a length of rope and stand students in pairs across from a partner who holds the other end of the rope. Then one student takes a length of rope and weaves it over and under until they get to the other side. You can also use lengths of fabric to make it easier to hold and see. Students in wheelchairs can have their rope tethered to their chair. You can sing a weaving song as you go.

Weaving, weaving, weaving in and out,
Over and under, over and under,
Let me hear you shout – hoi!

MAKING THE PIT

The pit where the sun lives is made by a circle of chairs turned around with a piece of lycra stretched over the backs. Students sit on the chairs and hold onto the lycra. Then the person playing the sun goes under the lycra and pushes a beach ball up against the fabric while the other students work together to keep the fabric stretched taut and not let the 'sun' escape. Then the person pushes a Swiss ball up against the fabric to symbolize the sun growing bigger, more powerful, and harder to contain. The students must struggle to keep the sun trapped while they act out a simple scene that we rehearse beforehand. The 'sun' calls out, 'Who is there?' and the students call back, 'Maui!' The 'sun' asks, 'What do you want?' and the students reply, 'We want you to slow down.' The 'sun' must then struggle to be free but finally give up and call out, 'Alright, I promise to slow down,' at which point the students draw back the lycra and the person playing the sun rises slowly to his feet, holding the ball above his head, and makes a slow movement across the circle.

The Windmaker

There came a time when a gale blew for nearly a month and the people began to starve. The berries were not ripening and no one could set sail to fish in such a wind. At last, one man volunteered to go and visit the Windmaker. He travelled far until he came to the source of the wind, a being with long arms that moved ceaselessly to and fro. The man commanded the Windmaker to stop moving and his tone was so sharp that the being stopped abruptly. The man then took his arms and tied them so that he could not move. The wind ceased immediately and everything became quiet. The man then returned to his people.

The skies became cloudless although the ocean still surged and the people could at last go out and fish to provide food for their children's hungry mouths. It wasn't long, though, before the sea became flatter than a millpond and dirt spread over its surface so that they could no longer fish. The people starved again and it was worse than before.

The man returned to the Windmaker and released his arms. He had to massage the life back into them and then teach the being how to produce the wind once more as he had forgotten. He took his long arms and swung them back and forth, turning this way and that way in a strange dance until at last the being remembered and began to dance of his own accord and light and life returned to his eyes. Then a gentle wind spread over the land and the water, bringing comfort to all the creatures. It washed the dirt from the water and piled it high in mounds on the shoreline so that the sea became clear and the fish good to eat. And the Windmaker sang out on the wind this message: 'I was created by the Great Spirit and it is not for you to say when I can blow and when I cannot. Be at peace and trust. The power to control the wind should not reside in a man's hands.'

Themes in the story

When I first began working in special education, I came across a teacher who used very unorthodox methods of managing her students' behaviour. This included putting soap in the mouth of a student who swore frequently and tying the sleeves of a student who touched other people's faces, so that he could not use his hands. Fortunately, this was the only time I came across a situation like this but it prompted me to use the story of the Windmaker about an individual deliberately disabled by another. I modified the version I read where the man chops off the arms of the Windmaker and in doing so got the idea of including some hand massage into the sessions with some students.

I had one class of students who were all teenagers with autism and quite difficult to engage. Most of them were very overweight, resistant to any movement, nonverbal and anxious. They were often uninterested in props, did not react to the masks and rarely showed any recognition of me. I worked on giving them a sensory experience of the story. Through this story, I discovered their enjoyment of hand massage. Some were initially reluctant but the support staff and I persevered as I discovered that one student began looking curiously at me while I massaged her hands. Another student gripped the teacher's wrist and tried to redirect her to continue as she began to move towards another student.

From then on, I included hand massage in every session, usually at the beginning, as it seemed to be performing the function of the warm-up. Some students were noticeably more alert for the duration of the session. I used a hypoallergenic base oil and varied the essential oils. In one session, I brought in a box of essential oils and offered them to the students to smell. We noted which were the favourites and which stimulated a negative response, a drawing back or a pushing away.

Ideas for the session

WINDMAKERS

These are plastic tubes which you rotate in order to produce a wind-like sound. They are available from toyshops and are not expensive but they do take quite a bit of coordination to make them work and you need space so that you avoid hitting other students. One in each hand can make the long arms of the Windmaker moving restlessly to and fro.

HAND DANCING

Hand dancing involves pairs facing each other. One person leads the movement, which is restricted to hands and arms. The other person mirrors the movement. In order to work, the movements need to be slow and simple, and synchronized so that it is difficult to distinguish who is leading and who is mirroring. Then the pairs swap over. Sometimes it helps to play slow, relaxing background music.

This activity worked beautifully in a class of profoundly disabled students where the support staff were paired with students, and with great sensitivity and gentleness mirrored the tiny movements some students could make or else supported elbows so that stiff fingers and hands could move.

In one class, we began with this exercise and as the students seemed to really enjoy it we extended it by using huge shirts (borrowed from the caretaker) that had the sleeves tied and weighted with sandbags. The students chose the music that best suited the windmaker from a selection of about ten pieces of classical and modern music. They then stood in a row like a number of wind turbines, swayed, and moved their hands from side to side in time with the music. This meant that the part where the man speaks so abruptly that the Windmaker ceases his movement was particularly dramatic as we timed it to occur with the stopping of the music and every other sound.

Within the consistent structure of warm-up, main event and closure, you can increase or decrease the amount of changeable elements in the session according to the students you have in the group. My experience is that once students are familiar with both me and the structure and have an idea of what to expect from drama sessions, their ability to be flexible noticeably improves.

5

Working as a Team

Egocentricity is a normal part of child development, but it tends to persist in children with an intellectual disability partly because of environmental factors. Research has shown the prevalence of vertical relationships as opposed to horizontal relationships in the lives of children with a learning disability (Hartup, 1989). Vertical relationships are those with someone older than themselves, an adult, usually a parent. Vertical relationships provide a range of basic social skills, but it is interactions with children more or less similar in age, referred to as horizontal relationships, which expose them to the complexities and competition needed to elaborate these basic skills.

In an inclusive setting (i.e. a mainstream school which included students with disabilities) children with a disability interacted with the teacher much more than children without a disability (Brophy and Hancock, 1985). This research showed that there was less exposure to interactions with peers, although it is these interactions which help children learn to adopt a less egocentric position and appreciate that others have needs and feelings too.

Chesner (1995) and Edwards (1998) have both expressed concern about the egocentricity of social development with this client group and how the environment can reinforce that. With an over-emphasis on interactions with teachers, care givers and other professionals, children become accustomed to being the focus of attention and having concessions made for their disability. Many special schools have different play areas in order to separate specific students who have conflicts with one another or different needs. While one can see the need for this type of segregation, opportunities to learn the skills needed to resolve conflict, one of the hallmarks of social competence, are further reduced. The kind of play observable in the special school playground is noticeably different to that of the mainstream junior school where there will be pockets of students interacting with one another in imaginative play and improvised games. In the special school playground, students tend not to interact with one another even when engaged in the same activity, for example, climbing on the jungle gym.

The drama therapy session provides a structured, safe environment in which to model and practise social skills. The format of the drama therapy session teaches and reinforces social skills with its emphasis on listening, turn taking and sharing. For some students, just the simple act of sitting and watching another student perform a task is a major achievement in itself. Demonstrating the appropriate skills of an audience is one of the learning objectives in the New Zealand national curriculum for drama and it is one that has profound implications for the learning disabled child who may not fully look at another person, especially a peer.

In normal childhood development, the movement from parallel playing, which is the ability to play alongside peers, to play that involves interacting with peers takes place at around 3 years old. An awareness of students' developmental age is important to an understanding of why they find interacting with peers problematic. It may simply be a matter of where they are developmentally and, with time, these skills may develop naturally. According to Piaget, social play, which involves rules and regulations, appears at around 7 years old. However, with some students, social competency deficits will continue over time, and interventions which address these issues are invaluable.

The four stories in this chapter give many physical opportunities for students to work alongside each other, interact with one another and participate in achieving a shared goal. For many students, close physical proximity is a challenge in itself. When I first began working in special schools, I would organize students to sit in a circle on the floor rather than in their chairs. I wanted drama to be a contrast to what they experienced in the rest of the timetable. Within a week, I had them sitting in their chairs again! Without personal space delineated by the chair, many students became aggressive defenders of their personal territory. They fidgeted constantly and some were visibly uneasy. In addition, sitting upright in the chair is often a cue to attentiveness – sitting on the floor seems to remind students of relaxing at home and their attentiveness suffers. So the chairs become the anchor, the safe haven where the student returns after coming into the acting space in the centre of the circle or from travels around the classroom.

I explored other possibilities for close physical proximity and found that lycra was an invaluable prop. With the students sitting on chairs, I ask them to grasp the lycra with both hands so that it is stretched across the circle.

Then I ask the teacher which two students would make a good combination to go underneath the lycra together. I nominate the two students and they crawl under the lycra while the rest of the group holds it taut over them. I then monitor them for any inappropriate touching like pinching and replaced the offending student if there are any problems. I return him to his seat, tell him clearly why he is being removed and let him try again later. I then ask the two students to extend their hands upwards so that we can see the shape of their fingers, or their toes or their spines. Some students holding the lycra instinctively reach out to grab and those supervising must be quick to show those students the gentle way to touch and praise gentle touching repeatedly. I always have quick looks under the lycra to check on the two underneath and certainly with a new group, everyone's turn is quite quick.

This is one way to teach students who are unfamiliar with physical proximity how to tolerate the presence of another and even enjoy it. It is of course vital that we model gentle touch in all our interactions with the students not just on those occasions when we are focusing on that particular skill.

You may find ways of incorporating this exercise with themes in the story you are using. A story set near the sea can have the students becoming fishes under the lycra, in a forest you may ask them to grow into something.

The Thunder of the Four Colours

Once, long ago, the land was flat and barren and nothing came from the soil.

So, the people decided to summon up the Thunder of the Four Colours to come from the four corners of the earth.

The colours came, bringing with them storm clouds, and when the clouds had gathered the people planted seeds in the earth.

Then they stamped and clapped and sang around the seeds and the rain began to fall.

As they carried on stamping and singing, a mountain began to grow and the land changed.

Flowers and plants began to grow.

Finally, the people called for the rainbow to make things beautiful.

Themes in the story

I love the simplicity of this story and its poem-like structure. It describes an almost mathematical configuration from whose alignment great transformation can take place. It describes the power of people working together with the elements to produce a fertile landscape. It is a story from the Native American Indians where a common theme is the interconnectedness of people and all living things. There are numerous dramatic possibilities from the creation of mountains to the appearance of the rainbow. This story is a good one to use with a new group. It contains many physical components like stamping and clapping and the concreteness of the elements make it understood by many children. The story has as its central image the coming together of diverse individuals in order to create something wonderful that transforms the landscape.

Ideas for the story

A good warm-up to use if you are emphasizing the colour aspect of the story and you want to make sure students can identify colours is one where you cut out pieces of coloured card and laminate them. Each student is given a card with a colour he can identify. The facilitator asks everyone with the colour 'red!' or whatever the colour may be to stand up. Some groups get quite competitive and make it into a game where the test is to see who is able to stand up first.

VARIATIONS

Staff can support students who are physically disabled to hold up the card or react when their colour is called. Staff can support students unsure about the names of colours by holding up an example of the colour while saying the name. From here, it is relatively simple to discard the cards in favour of fabrics in the main four colours. Students choose which colour they would like to be (it helps to have plenty of fabrics so that more than one student can play the colour of their choice) and identify a corner which they want to stand in.

SUMMONING THE FOUR COLOURS

I made up a simple chant to accompany the part where the four colours are at the four corners of the earth waiting to be summoned. It goes like this:

Red, red, rain on my head, will you come down now, red?
Blue, blue, will you come too, will you come down now, blue?

Green, green, wash the earth clean. Will you come down now, green?
Yellow, yellow, do you want to follow, will you come down now, yellow?

As each colour is called, the student or students playing the colour call out 'Yes,' as loud and as clearly as they can and everyone else applauds, stamps and drums. In this way, we provide a lot of positive reinforcement for inclusion in the group experience.

PLANTING THE SEEDS

When everyone is assembled in the centre of a circle, we are ready to plant the seeds. With some groups it may be more appropriate to use the sand tray (see page 45). With students who can make ball shapes, you can get them to curl up small, cover them with a dark cloth (for seeds need darkness to germinate) and have other students be the rain with gentle drumming of fingers on backs or with the rainmaker (see page 35 for a description of a rainmaker). You encourage students to 'grow' up towards the light, whisking off the black fabrics at the same time. Some students may be able to tell you what they have grown into. You may have rehearsed this in the warm-up with a discussion around what kinds of things grow. Whatever the case, accept the contribution from the student regardless of how appropriate it is – 'grass' is wonderful, but 'sausage' and 'racing car' are great too. It is incredibly difficult for many students to recognize members of the same group, so asking them to identify examples of things that grow is a really tall order. The main thing is that they have responded to a verbal cue 'What are you?' with a response of their own initiative and we want to encourage this as much as possible.

MAKING THE RAINBOW

This involves adding extra colours to the four colours to make a rainbow. Have long lengths of fabric that the students can hold across the circle or tie together to make a rainbow. Students can waft the fabrics up and down while we sing the rainbow song. This is a call and response song which is simple enough to vary if need be.

Verse
A rainbow has colours.
It's sparkling and bright.
It fills every corner
With rays of pure light.

Chorus
Hey witchitawa.
Witchitawa.
Witchi, witchi tawa.
Witchitawa.

Verse
We all are that rainbow.
In our own special way.
Brightening up the classroom
Every single day.

Chorus
Hey witchitawa.
Witchitawa.
Witchi, witchi tawa.
Witchitawa.

The bog people

The bog people live in the bog and hate the light. They love jewels and their favourite pastime is to lie in wait on dark nights and accost travellers whose journey takes them through the bog and steal all their jewels.

Eventually people realize that the bog people never strike on moonlit nights and so most people arrange their travel to coincide with moonlight. This makes the bog people very unhappy and they plot what to do.

Eventually they decide to capture the moon so that the nights will always be dark. They set out to clear a patch of bog of weeds and algae until it is as clear as a looking-glass and then they lie in wait for the moon to come up.

Some time later, the moon rises and it is a little sliver of moon as fine as a baby's fingernail. They all croon to the moon to come down and look at herself in the glass as they know she is very vain.

She catches sight of herself, leaves off her ascent, and instead comes down to the earth to have a closer look. When she is very close, the bog people leap up and catch her in a net.

All becomes darkness and the bog people are overjoyed. They dance and caper about and are able to catch many travellers unawares who trusted the moonlight to lend them a safe passage through the bog.

At first it all seems to be satisfactory to the bog people. However, they very soon realize that the moon is growing bigger and bigger underneath the net and proving harder and harder to keep ensnared. Until, finally, on the night she is full, she bursts free of their trap and goes sailing up into the sky once more.

Themes in the story

There is something Gollum-like about the bog people who live in the dark and love jewels. The capturing of the moon mirrors in some ways Maui's capture of the sun in the Maori story (see Chapter 4) although in this case the bog people are unable to hang on to it as it follows its inevitable path of growing to fullness. The moon's vanity almost proves its undoing, a common theme in traditional stories.

Ideas for the story

I use a bag of costume jewellery as the prop and give students the chance to dress up and admire themselves. This involves a great deal of sharing and teamwork. I explain that the jewels are mine from home and I want them to take care of them and not snatch them from each other and never, ever pull a piece of jewellery off over someone's head.

The next group endeavour is the clearing of the pond to make it like a mirror. For this, I often use a piece of lycra which I cover with leaves and burrs and dry stuff from the garden. Some students particularly relish this part of the story and become very absorbed in cleaning the 'pond'. It is similar to the enjoyment they get from clearing up the shredded paper in 'Hemi and the whale' (see below).

The next part involves crooning at the moon to come down for which I use a special song, which we all sing together, to the tune of 'Rock-a-bye baby'. It goes like this:

Come down sweet moony, come have a look.
Come see your beauty, here in the brook.
Look at your sweet face, see how you smile.
Come closer, dear moony, stay for a while.

Sometimes I use my 'scary' masks for the bog people. Once, I used plain white masks that meant everyone could have a go at the same time and one class made masks with their teacher and used them. The group must work together holding the lycra in order to throw it over the 'moon' at the same time. A count of three is a good cue and students can begin to anticipate. The moon is one person or a group of people who have to curl up small and grow bigger at the same time. I often set up a chair or set of chairs to which they can 'fly' up to symbolize their return to the loftiness of the sky.

Hemi and the whale

Hemi is a small boy who lives near the sea and every morning he gets up early and goes down to the seashore to explore and look at the sea and every day there is something different to look at – it is always changing.

This morning there was something terrible on the beach that made Hemi's heart flip over. It was a whale! Lying on the sand, so still. Hemi ran over to look at the whale thinking it was dead, but he saw the blowhole open and close and he realized the whale was still breathing. So, he ran, ran back up to the house to his nanny calling, 'Kura, kura, get water, quick. There's a whale on the beach!' He ran and got buckets and started filling them with water but they were very heavy and it took all his strength not to spill the water on the way.

Meanwhile, his nanny, looking out the window, saw what was happening and called his granddad. His granddad called the neighbour who called another neighbour and very quickly there was a whole group of people running up and down the beach carrying buckets of water trying to keep the whale wet until the incoming tide could float it back out to sea again. Someone brought bed sheets to cover the whale and help to keep its skin moist. Finally the tide came in and began to wash up against the mighty animal. Hemi was right by its head when it opened one unblinking, liquid black eye. 'Hold on, whale,' said Hemi 'you'll soon be home.'

Then everyone worked together to support the whale. Some pulled on the sheets to steer the beast and others pushed from behind, struggling in the foamy water and the wet sand. Finally, they felt the life come back into the whale. Its body shuddered and it took a massive breath in through its blowhole then blew out again violently. It nosed down into the tide and slipped off the sheets and the helping hands and a big cheer went up as it flicked its flukes and began to swim back out to sea.

Hemi stayed on the sea shore long after everyone else had gone, watching the waves and scanning the horizon for his whale. Finally his nanny came down and laid a hand on his shoulder and said, 'I'm proud of you, boy.' They walked back to the house together.

Themes in the story

This is a very simple short story but I have had great fun with it, and its central scenario, that of rescuing the beached whale, is an ideal one for having the class work together as a team. The story is local to where I live in Auckland where the sea is never far away and most kids are familiar with images of whales stranding themselves; if they haven't direct experience they may have seen pictures on the local news. It could easily be categorized as an unlikely-heroes story, but I have included it here as enacting the story gives numerous opportunities for everyone to work together. The child in the story is the one who sees the beached whale and mobilizes the community to save it. The story contains the theme of the child being more connected or aware of its relationship to the natural world while adults may be too wrapped up in what they are doing to notice. Hemi's ability to assist others is affirmed at the end of the story. Chapter 3 deals with the importance of helping others in detail.

Ideas for the session

I have an inflatable whale, which is fun to include in a warm-up. However, for the students to really get the idea they are helping to save another living being, I find it important to use a well-loved staff member to be the whale. I remember doing this story with a class of 7-year-olds. Their teacher was a very loving, male teacher who was more than happy to lie down and be rescued. One of the students was quite new to the school and had been very shy and nervous in drama and all the group activities. However, when Trevor lay down, she lay down beside him and he put his arm around her and they made the whale together. On that occasion, we used shredded paper for the water. It is relatively easy to come by (the school office is a good source) and reasonably easy to clear up and some groups enjoy the clearing up almost as much as the story. I like to get as much as possible, at least a couple of big, rubbish bags-full. It doesn't matter if students pick up handfuls to put on the whale although one group I worked with was able to make a line and pass buckets of 'water' down to the whale. Encourage the children all to work together so if we are all pushing the whale back out to sea we are all pushing in the same direction. Some children can run and get 'water' while others pat and reassure the whale.

The praise from the nanny at the end of the story is important. Often students cheer when the 'whale' begins to swim off and they can become very absorbed in clearing up the classroom and putting the shredded paper back in the bags. However, in order to emphasize that they have done a job well I do a group back pat as a closure exercise. Here we stand in a circle facing the same way and raise one hand and bring it down gently on the back or shoulder of the person in front and give them a 'well done' pat.

This is a good story to storyboard for use with autistic students as it is very simple and the images are relatively easy to access (for more details, see Chapter 12).

The healing waters

A village was enduring the worst winter for many years. There was a terrible sickness and people were dying. The people knew that they would have to find the healing waters in order to save the sick people. This would mean they would have to go out into the wilderness to search. The wilderness was cold and full of wild animals.

People were afraid, but a group of brave people said they would go. They wrapped up in their warmest clothes and set off. The wind blew snow in their faces and it was very harsh and cold. They walked for three days until they came upon a cave where they could shelter from the wind and snow. Inside the cave was warm and dry. They crawled in and immediately fell asleep because they were so tired.

As they slept, the wilderness animals came and looked at their sleeping faces. They knew they were in great danger from the cold. They saw they had kind faces. They didn't want the people to die. Therefore, they sent up a prayer to the Great Spirit to save the people and the Great Spirit heard their prayer. The Great Spirit sent the people a dream in which they heard a voice saying 'dig!'

When they awoke, they stretched and yawned and then someone said, 'I had the strangest dream. I heard a voice saying "dig!"'

And someone else said, 'I heard a voice saying "dig!"' and another and another. So, they decided to dig. The ground was very cold and hard and they only had their bare hands but they kept going and the ground got softer and easier to dig. Suddenly they heard a big rumble from beneath the earth and all of a sudden the earth cracked open and a huge spurt of warm spring water soaked everyone.

They tasted some of the water. It tasted good and they felt much better. They wondered, 'Could this be the healing waters?' So, they tried it out on cuts and bruises and the cuts and bruises disappeared. They were so happy.

They made pots out of the earth and filled them with water to take back to the village but as they were leaving the cave someone tripped and spilt theirs on the snow and an amazing thing happened. The snow began to melt in front of them all the way back to the village, which made their journey home much easier. They arrived back to the village not only with the healing waters but with the spring as well.

Ever after, the people who had gone on the journey were known as the mothers and the fathers of the healing waters.

Themes in the story

When I originally heard this story, it was called 'Nekumonta's dream' and was about one man making the journey to find the healing waters to save his sick wife and others in the village. Yet when I began enacting it with students, I found there were a large number who wanted to make the arduous journey together and as working together was a skill I wanted to develop, it made sense to change the story to be about a group endeavour.

The story has a very strong theme of self-sacrifice and putting the needs of the group ahead of personal needs. In the West, the prevailing myth is of the importance and supremacy of the individual and this is the bedrock of democratic societies where self-determination and self-sufficiency are seen as evidence of emotional growth and maturity. Independence, self-reliance, autonomy, and separation from parents, particularly one's mother, are considered therapeutic goals. However, many cultures emphasize the importance of subservience of personal gains for the good of the community. Although Western democracies ostensibly prize individualism, there is a hunger for the kind of heroism displayed in both world wars where many people felt that their own needs were subservient to the needs of the greater good.

Ideas for the story

Some students enjoy looking after their 'sick' classmates and getting them pillows and blankets to keep them warm while they are away. I have used ice cubes to remind students of 'cold', which is a hard thing to imagine when you are not cold. Ice packs work as well and are not as messy. I bought lengths of cleaning cloths, which were sold in tubes, to use as hoods that people could wear over their heads and pull up over their faces. I used the thin rope for us all to hold on to as we were in a blizzard and could not afford to lose anyone.

Staff can be very creative with ideas of how to evoke a blizzard in the middle of summer. In one profoundly disabled group I worked with, a staff member loved spraying fine mist from a bottle in order for the students to understand water. I think it can work really well sprayed onto the palm of a person's hand rather than their face.

I made the journey from the village in the centre of the semi-circle over to two tables I set up in the opposite end of the room covered with a blanket to make the cave. It's usually fine for 'sleeping' under but you usually have to move out into the bigger space to do the digging.

The rainmaker can be used to play at healing people's hurts. Some students will enter into the fantasy and point out bruises and cuts for you or another student to 'heal'. I ask them, 'Does that feel better?' and they will invariably say, 'Yes'.

I usually use playdoh for the little pots the villagers make to carry the water back to the village. The return to the village with the precious water is a time of celebration and students can go round administering to the 'sick'. When everyone is assembled, it is a good time to sing a song. I use a Native American song that is easy to remember. I let a student beat the rhythm with a drum while we all stamp in a circle.

> The earth, the air, the fire, the water, return, return, return, return.
> The earth, the air, the fire, the water, return, return, return, return.
> I-A-I-A-I-A-I-A
> I-O-I-O-I-O-I-O
> I-A-I-A-I-A-I-A
> I-O-I-O-I-O-I-O.
> The earth, the air, the fire, the water, return, return, return, return.
> The earth, the air, the fire, the water, return, return, return, return.

What you are aiming to do with these stories is give students an awareness of how much can be achieved when we work together as a team. What we aim to give in the sessions is an experience of how pleasant and fun it can also be.

6

Trickery and Stealing

The heroes in this group of stories are all children or young people. Most of them are profoundly irritating to the adults around them. Jack is described as a 'lazy feckless boy', Maui is notoriously perverse and trouble-making, Raven is a thorn in the Shaman's side. The children in the King Arthur story are lacking in any individual characteristics. They are just poor children. I take responsibility for that as I devised the story myself, so the characters do not come from a tradition the way the other characters do.

Straightaway we are giving many students a hero with whom they can identify. The heroes' individual situations are similar in that they are all in dire need, in need of food, warmth, shelter, fire. The stories are clearly about survival and the heroes of these stories do what they need to do in order to survive. They steal. There are twin themes of trickery and stealing in all of the stories. I have never had any moral objections to the stories' use in special schools. Staff know that I am not teaching students how to steal nor saying that stealing is OK. The stealing is not prompted by greed but necessity. In the King Arthur story, once the children get what they need, the treasures of the tree are no longer available to them.

However, for some of these heroes, a love of danger and mischief overrides common sense. Jack is similar to Maui in that he thirsts for adventure even when the need no longer exists. Once in possession of the golden-egg-laying hen, Jack's financial problems are effectively over. Yet he returns to the giant's house two more times until he is nearly caught. Maui returns to his grandmother as she becomes angrier and angrier and the threat to his safety increases. There is a kind of thrill-seeking behaviour here, a pushing of the boundaries which a lot of children and adolescents identify with.

Many people have stolen when children and most would never dream of stealing as an adult. This is not just because of a finer ethical sense but often because there is no need. As adults, we have resources at our disposal in order to get the things we need and want. However, children rarely control their own resources and they have to find other, covert ways of getting what they want. The stories involve stealth, the ability to control one's impulses and manage one's own fear, as well as being able to run fast and having a good sense of timing.

The children in the stories triumph over adults who are drunk, asleep, or allow themselves to be tricked. In Raven's case, he evokes magical powers and transforms himself in order to escape the old man's wrath. The children outwit the adults and this makes the stories very attractive to students. Having control over one's fear is a theme in many children's games, some of which I describe below.

When you set up the conditions where the student can trick you, you are letting him be seen as cleverer than you are and for many students, this is a very potent and unfamiliar experience.

King Arthur's gold

Two poor children were playing in the woods close to their home. They climbed a huge oak tree and stood on one of the highest branches looking out over the countryside. All of a sudden, the branch broke and the children toppled down inside the body of the tree, which was hollow. They fell down and down until they found themselves inside the base of the tree and facing a huge rock which was blocking the entrance of a cave. Together, they put their shoulders against the rock, pushed, and pushed until they managed to move it out of the way and they could see a tunnel that ended in a cave. There was a lamp flickering and they were very curious. They crawled on their hands and knees and emerged in a strange room with the most amazing sight ahead of them. The room was huge and lit by oil lamps that burned eternally. In the centre of the room was a huge treasure chest full of gold and jewels spilling out from the top.

Surrounding the chest was a group of a dozen men all dressed identically in sumptuous armour. All were lying in a circle with their feet pointing towards the chest and all seemed fast asleep. One was dressed even more richly than the others and on his chest, clasped by both hands, lay a wonderful sword. The children recognized the man as King Arthur and the sword as Excalibur. They guessed the other men were his loyal knights who legend had it had not died but waited in readiness for Britain's darkest hour.

The children knew that it was most important that they did not wake the knights, but they were fascinated by the gold and knew that even a little would transform their lives and that of their poor widowed mother. As carefully as they could, they crept past the knights towards the chest, lifted the lid and took some gold, just enough to fill their pockets. Then quietly, quietly, they crept out again without making a sound and made their way back along the tunnel towards the roots of the tree, where they climbed up out into the bright sunshine.

Their mother was overjoyed to see them and the gold made sure they never went hungry. However, no matter how hard they searched, they were not able to find the old oak tree and the secrets contained in its dark roots ever again.

This is a story I devised in response to a need from a fragment I heard somewhere: I was working with a class of 6-to 7-year-olds and the physiotherapist had asked if I could integrate climbing, falling, crawling and pushing into their drama sessions. I had also recently acquired a wonderful suit of armour which I wanted to use as a prop. The story is from an apocryphal story about King Arthur which maintains that King Arthur did not die but is asleep somewhere in the Malvern Hills, with a handful of his best-loved knights. He is waiting for a time when England needs him most and he will arise and come to its rescue. There are shadows of the Grimms' Tinderbox story which itself includes many elements of Aladdin and another children's story I vaguely remember about finding treasure and only taking a small amount. But it was through this story that I discovered the enduring popularity of stealth games that have many variations and can be played with a variety of different abilities. Part of the attraction is that the games enable the acting out and legitimizing of the forbidden which is immensely attractive to children. They also allow the child to appear to be cleverer than the adult.

With this story, I devised a simple version that most students can play. As usual, I made sure that the task was modelled. I lay as King Arthur with the sword on my chest and the treasure box (a plastic lunchbox) between my feet. Inside the box was a length of gold material that the student had to filch without waking me up. If the student made a sound (and of course, I made allowances according to the ability of the student to control his sounds), I sat bolt upright and made an ominous sound. In the quiet of the game, it was extremely startling, and students usually got a fright and then laughed. If they managed to get the 'gold' without waking 'King Arthur', they had to say, 'Wakey wakey' and I would wake up and look suitably astounded. Everyone would clap. The game can be played with different degrees of sophistication. With some groups, it is enough that the student goes straight over and grabs the cloth. With other groups, I insist on them doing it quietly.

There are a number of stealth games that can be played outside the context of the story and which I use for warm-ups in groups where we are devising our own stories. For more details, see Chapter 11.

Sword play and sword fighting

The plastic sword available in most toyshops is a wonderful prop to use. I like the swords that have a scabbard and make a satisfying sound as they come out of the sheath. Again, the issue of trust is paramount as it is in activities involving the axe. Many teachers would be reluctant to give a toy sword to their students. However, drama affords the opportunity to do many things unavailable to the student in real life.

Activities with the sword teach impulse control, fine tune motor skills and give, especially the male students, the opportunity to express aggressive energy in a controlled environment. Many students need to learn how to manage their energy and the sword is part of a courtly tradition that taught young men to do just that. The rules are important and the activity is broken down systematically into a three-stage sequence that gives me the chance to see that everyone is going to abide by the rules. The sequence comprises taking the sword by the handle, drawing off the scabbard, and holding the sword at arm's length in an upright position. It is followed by praise for having 'good sword control'. I then usually model fighting with a staff member and this involves moving everyone back from the action, squaring up to one another and hitting each other's swords. We make appropriate sounds when our swords are hit. After three or four hits, I start to struggle and once on the ground, my opponent lifts his sword above his head in a victory salute.

Then it is time for the students to have a turn with me. Staff support is provided when a student is physically unable to aim his sword to hit my sword. If a student fails to hit my sword and instead hits me due to inattention to the task, I will ask him to sit down and maybe try him later on. I have never encountered a student who has used the exercise to be vindictive. It just has not happened.

For reasons of safety, I do not usually pair one student with another. In one special school, I had a class that had three teenagers with conduct disorder. They had a tendency to be both verbally and physically aggressive and were very reluctant to engage in many drama activities, initially because of what appeared to be an almost pathological fear of being humiliated or looking 'uncool'. I taught them drama fighting and we practised stage slaps and having heated arguments with one another that I froze just prior to actual physical contact. The activity momentarily released in the boys a wonderful youthful enthusiasm where all the studied cynicism burned off. They appeared much more relaxed and it created a positive relationship with me. In this way, drama provides a unique opportunity for students to channel and express aggression without anyone getting hurt.

Jack and the beanstalk

Jack lived with his mother and they were very poor. His mother found it very hard to put any checks on Jack and consequently he was a lazy, feckless boy. The time came when they found that they had no money, no food in the cupboard and nothing left to sell. Nothing, that is, except their lovely dun cow. Jack's mother was heartbroken to part with her, but seeing that she had no choice she put Jack in charge of the matter, instructing him to take Daisy to market and get the best possible price for her so that they could at least eat that evening.

Jack set off in great high spirits, but in the heat of the day he soon became bored and tired. So when he came upon the butcher (who knew him for the lad that he was) he was more than happy to hand over the cow for a handful of beans that the wily butcher gave him. Delighted, he returned home to tell his mother.

At the sight of the beans, his mother finally lost all patience. She threw the beans out of the window and was in great distress; she and Jack retired to bed without any supper.

In the morning when Jack awoke, he feared it was still night for the room was dark although the birds were singing. He rushed out to the garden and soon discovered why. The beans had miraculously sprouted and taken root during the night and grown at a prodigious rate. Each trunk was thicker than a man's thigh and they curled around each other almost creating a ladder that stretched farther than the eye could see, way above the clouds. Jack immediately decided to climb the beanstalk and, ignoring his mother's entreaties, he started to climb.

Jack climbed for some hours until he reached the top, quite exhausted. There he found a barren landscape, not a bird singing nor a blade of grass stirring. He walked along a road until he came to a house with a woman standing at the door. She was surprised to see a human as it was well known that her husband was a giant, but Jack persuaded her to let him in for some food and drink, telling her she could hide him in the oven. She was a soft-hearted woman and agreed. She led Jack through the house and into the warm kitchen to have a good feed.

Suddenly, the ground began to shake with the sound of the giant returning. 'Quick, in the oven!' said the wife just as the giant burst through the door.

'Fee fie fo fum, I smell the blood of a little one,' said the giant, but his wife reassured him.

Jack spied on the giant through the door of the oven. He saw him eat and drink a huge amount and then call for his hen. This was a hen that laid golden eggs and the giant amused himself playing with the hen all evening until he fell asleep.

As soon as the coast was clear, Jack sneaked out of the oven and, tucking the hen under one arm, he made his escape. Back home with his mother they soon became rich with the sale of the golden eggs.

However, Jack had a yearning to try his luck in the giant's house once more. So, disguising himself and ignoring his mother's tearful entreaties, he made his way back up the beanstalk.

The giant's wife was reluctant to take Jack in, disguised as he was, as she had suffered greatly after the theft of the hen. Eventually she let him in and hid him in the lumber cupboard. When the giant came home he said, 'Fee fie fo fum, I smell the blood of a little one,' but she made an excuse and he settled down to eat.

When he had finished he called for his money bags and occupied himself counting his gold. When Jack was sure the giant was asleep, he crept out and grasped the bags as quietly as he could. Luckily he was able to make his escape down the beanstalk.

It was three years before Jack thought to return to the giant's house. He went secretly, in disguise, and found the giant's wife standing at the door as before. She took a lot of persuading to let him in, but eventually she did and concealed him in the copper.

When the giant returned he said, 'Fee fie fo fum, I smell the blood of a little one.' No amount of reassuring could convince him otherwise and he began to thoroughly search the room. Jack was terrified. At one point the giant stood with his hand upon the copper – but at the last minute he turned aside and settled down to eat his supper.

When he had finished he called his wife to fetch the harp and she brought the most amazing instrument that played itself. The music was so sweet that the giant was lulled to sleep. Jack crept out of his hiding place and seized the harp, but it was enchanted and cried out, 'Master, master!' Immediately the giant awoke and if he had not been so drunk he would have caught Jack in a flash. Instead, he went reeling after him as Jack sped away to the beanstalk as fast as his legs could carry him. He was first on the beanstalk and as he descended he called out to his mother, 'Mother, quick, fetch the axe!' When Jack reached the bottom of the beanstalk, the giant was still a long way up and a few vigorous chops managed to bring down the beanstalk and the giant with it. The giant fell down and was killed instantly. Jack embraced his mother who was so relieved to see him and from that day on, he strove to be a good and dutiful son, which he eventually managed to be.

Jack and his mother lived happily ever after.

Themes in the story

The story contains the theme of the unlikely hero; he is the one least expected to win the day. He's a boy described as lazy, he is not engaged in the life he shares with his mother, but the journey up the beanstalk catapults him into an alternative reality, one where his personal qualities of courage and audacity bring great rewards. He is raised by his mother, who indulges and spoils him. There is no mention of his father.

In the Grimms' version, the giant was known to his father and had killed him in full view of Jack's mother who 'was stupefied with horror and grief, and was motionless' (Opie and Opie, 1980, p.217). Her fear of the giant was the reason she never revealed the truth to her son. This version presents the killing as justification for Jack availing himself of as many of the giant's possessions as he can. On one level, it is describing a mother with a history of great trauma struggling to raise her son on her own.

It is certainly very hard for single mothers to give children, particularly boys, the boundaries they need in order to successfully manage their drives and impulses. Often we have male students who are difficult to engage, easily bored, and thrill seeking. They respond much better to teaching methods that are kinesthetic and interactive. They prefer to be active and any didactic teaching has to be done in small amounts whenever the opportunity arises. It is another reason why drama therapy is so successful in engaging them.

Ideas for the story

HIDE AND SEEK

You can role-play the giant and ask the students to all hide in different places in the room, then do the rhyme 'fee fie fo fum' and come and find them. Support staff can accompany those students who are more nervous. I never involve masks as the process of hiding and being sought is scary enough. If you feel that this is too confrontational for your students you can use a little doll to be Jack and the students can take turns hiding him somewhere in the room. The students' job is to indicate when we are getting warmer, close to finding Jack, or colder, moving away.

DISGUISE

The story mentions that Jack had to disguise himself so that the giant's wife would not recognize him. I have had great fun bringing a selection of costumes and wigs and seeing how much we can disguise ourselves. It is an activity that is enjoyable for most abilities as long as time is taken with nonverbal students to ascertain their wishes and respond sensitively. The more staff become involved the better, not just in helping students dress up but being willing to dress up themselves. An eyebrow pencil can draw on freckles or moustaches, wigs can be made out of wool or hats used to cover hair. Some students like to look at themselves in a mirror and you may want to take some pictures to admire later.

A variation that can be used with more able students is the game 'Good afternoon, your majesty'. Here one person sits in a chair with his back to the others who sit about three metres away. The teacher silently nominates someone from the group, who has to call out, 'Good afternoon, your majesty,' in a disguised voice. If the person guesses correctly, the two have to change places. If he guesses incorrectly, someone else has a turn calling out.

THE FARMER WANTS A WIFE

This is a traditional children's game that many younger groups love. At a very basic level, it has the beginnings of role-play. Students are chosen to be characters but all they have to do is stand in the centre of the circle. The game begins with one student in the centre of the circle and everyone else singing, 'The farmer wants a wife, the farmer wants a wife, hi ho the derry-o, the farmer wants a wife.' That student then chooses someone from the circle to stand beside him and be his 'wife' and we sing, 'And the wife wants a child, the wife wants a child, hi ho the derry-o, the wife wants a child.' And so on through nurse and on to cat or whatever combination you want, ending with, 'And we all pat the dog, we all pat the dog, hi ho the derry-o, we all pat the dog.' You can vary the characters and always make sure that there are enough for everyone to be chosen.

CLIMBING THE BEANSTALK

See Chapter 3 for details of rope climbing. For stealth games see above. In one class, students had to creep up on a sleeping giant and take a set of bells hanging from a wooden frame representing the harp. It was a major achievement to move the frame without the bells making a sound.

Maui's search for fire

Maui cannot resist dousing the campfire as he and his brothers sleep around it in the open and so he is forced to go into the underworld to steal fire from his grandmother, Mahuika. He makes the perilous journey into the underworld and comes across Mahuika, sitting in the darkness; her children are her fiery fingertips blazing in the gloom. When he first sees her, Maui is very afraid as she is a fearsome and beautiful figure, but he knows what he must do. So he summons all his courage and calls out, 'Old woman, will you give me some fire?' She asks him who he is and he says, 'It is I, Maui, your grandson.' When Mahuika is satisfied that he is indeed her grandchild she gives him one of her fingernails and he sets off back to the upper air.

However, on the way, his trickster's ways overcome him and he resolves to take all his grandmother's fire so he douses the fingernail in some water and heads back to Mahuika. Again and again, he asks her for fire and she acquiesces, although each time she gets angrier and angrier until finally, there is only one fingernail left. Mahuika suddenly realizes what Maui is up to and her fury arises and she throws her last piece of fire at him and it pursues him through the underworld. 'Run, Maui, run!'

He bursts out into the world and the world begins to burn. He passes through the forests and the trees catch fire. He runs to the river but the river begins to boil. Just as the flames are about to catch him he turns himself into an eagle and calls on Tawhirimatea, the god of winds and storms, to send the rain. The rain pours down in floods and the fire is extinguished. The last remaining flame hid itself in the kaikomako tree and there it remains to this day, in its dry wood, waiting to be released when two pieces are rubbed together.

Themes in the story

Maui is a trickster demi-god whose destructiveness is tempered by his creativity. He is the mythical being responsible for fishing up Aotearoa or New Zealand from the ocean; he invented the fish basket for catching eels, and created the dog, the only domestic animal of his people.

The concept of whanau, or extended family, replaces the nuclear family in Maori society. Grandparents traditionally played an important part in the raising of a child and were accorded great respect. Maui tricks and robs both his grandmothers and is extremely disrespectful to them. His actions are often shocking – he deliberately starves his other grandmother in order to take her magic jawbone – or incomprehensible, as in the dousing of the fire.

Once he has one fiery fingernail he returns again and again as the danger from his grandmother's anger increases. It seems he cannot resist pushing the boundaries as far as they will go, with dramatic results. The chase takes place amidst the tumult of the four elements of fire, water, air and earth. Maui's actions upset the natural world but bring far-reaching benefits for the people. The story contains the theme of an individual confronting a powerful supernatural being in order to secure greater autonomy for the community. Until now, fire is a precious commodity jealously guarded, whose source lies elsewhere in the underworld, with grandmother. Maui's actions release fire into the world and make it readily available to everyone.

Ideas for the story
GRANDMOTHER'S FOOTSTEPS

'Grandmother' stands at the front of the class with her back turned and students have to creep up on her to try to touch her. Every time she turns round, they have to freeze and if she sees anyone moving, they have to go back and start again. There are many variations on this game.

For grandmother's costume I had a long black wig and a black cloak and for her fiery fingernails I used red feathers sellotaped onto a willing staff member's fingers. The student knows that 'grandmother' is getting angrier each time he returns and he has to get ready to pluck the last fingernail, as he knows she will give chase. In one classroom we created a landscape for Maui to run through which was around the perimeter of the room, having pushed the furniture into the centre of the room. Maui ran around the perimeter while other students were the forests on fire, the river on fire, the storms and the final section being the dry kaikomako trees. We used fabrics, strips of paper and water sprayers to convey the experience. We chanted, 'Run, Maui, run!' and the student had to get to the end before the fire caught up with him.

Relays were an excellent way to convey the experience of Maui running through a constantly changing landscape. Here students stand in a line with the first person holding a feather, a stick, or a red cloth to represent the fire. He passes this over his head to the next person who passes it under his legs and so on down the line. When the last person has the 'fire', he has to run to the front to begin the process again until everyone has had a turn being at the front. With enough students, you can have races between two competing lines.

Raven and the light

The winter is the darkest anyone can remember and no one knows why.

The people ask the shaman to perform a ritual to restore the light. He begins to drum and dance and puts himself into a trance, but it is just as dark as before. One of the young boys in the village claims that he can find the light. The shaman is furious at the boy's presumptuousness and banishes him from the village.

The boy has to travel alone into the wilderness, into the dark and snow. After a while, he comes upon some arctic chickens. He asks them, 'Can you tell me who has taken the light?'

The chickens reply that they do not know but they tell him to ask the caribou who are grazing in herds all along the wide snowy wastes. He travels on until he finds the herds. He asks them, 'Can you tell me who has taken the light?'

They tell him that they don't know but that he should ask the wolves who are roaming in packs. So off he goes trudging through the snow and sure enough, as he approaches a pack of wolves he can see the glimmer of something over the horizon. From a distance, he calls to the wolves, 'Can you tell me who has taken the light?'

They nod and gesture over the ridge and off he goes with the light getting stronger and stronger every step of the way.

As he comes over the ridge he sees where the light is coming from. There is a tent pitched with an old man sitting in front of it carving, and bobbing around, tied to the tent, is the sun.

The boy approaches the old man warily for he knows he is in the presence of great magic and the old man does not look very friendly. The old man looks up and growls, 'What do you want?'

The boy knows he cannot ask for the sun and must find a way of taking it, so he humbly asks the old man if he will teach him how to carve. The man glares at him and looks at him intently then nods and disappears inside the tent to get his tools. The boy takes the opportunity to grab the sun and begins to run off with it. The old man gives chase and for an old man he is very fast as he starts to gain on the boy, but the boy throws the sun up into the sky and, turning three times, he sprouts wings and flies up after it in the form of a raven.

And that is how the sun was returned to the world and how a boy became the character we know as Raven.

Themes in the story

This Inuit story about the boy later known as Raven follows a familiar pattern to a number of myths that start with a land sunk in darkness – someone has taken the light. He has similarities with Maui in that he has the ability to shape shift. In the Native American Indian tradition there is no major dividing line between the world of people and animals and many characters were not just named after certain animals but shared their characteristics. This story describes the point at which the boy assumes his raven nature and is known ever after as Raven. It is a rite of passage story where the immature young boy, through participation in a wilderness journey and confronting his fears, grows into his powers and is transformed into another being.

Ideas in the story

I had a fearful-looking wooden mask from Bali that I used for the shaman. I gave the students shakers and they had to create a rhythm in order to put the shaman into a trance. I put on the mask and stood still until I could hear a rhythm being played when I would begin to move. For some students, who found the mask quite scary, there was great delight in being able to make it move with the use of the shaker.

I used masks for the chickens, caribou and wolves. I used a pop-up tent for the old man's tent that the younger children loved. In fact, it was quite difficult to get some students out of the tent! I used a bright yellow helium balloon for the sun and tied it loosely to the top of the tent. I devised a simple scene between the boy and the old man that consisted of the boy approaching the old man carving outside his tent. The old man says, grumpily and suspiciously, 'What do you want?' The boy replies innocently, 'Will you teach me how to carve?' The old man looks him up and down for a second then disappears into the tent. The boy takes the opportunity to grab the sun and run.

It was in an enactment of this story that I realized that the lines between story and reality had become blurred with distressing results. We were enacting the part where the boy tentatively approaches the old man who growls at him. Emma had opted to play the role of the boy and was the first to have a go. I played the old man and sat on a stool outside the pop-up tent that was my arctic home. Emma was the brightest student in her class and very familiar with both the drama sessions and myself. I had no concerns about her going first. However, after I had growled at her, 'What do you want?' she began to look visibly upset and was unable to do her line about wanting to learn how to carve. The teacher began to prompt her with the line but I could see that she was frightened rather than forgetful. I said, 'Emma, look, it's me, Paula,' and I smiled at her, but she would not make eye contact or look at me. I then asked one of the teacher aides who I knew she liked to stand with her and approach me again and this time I moderated the amount of grumpiness I injected in the role.

This time Emma was able to look at me but the teacher aide delivered her line and she was still very nervous about creeping up and snatching the sun tied to my tent, so I let a few other people have a turn while she watched. Finally, she started to giggle and when I asked her if she wanted another go, she was able to do the part in its entirety. She was laughing and confident and her relief was palpable and I knew that she had met a very great challenge in the session, that of confronting a bad tempered, threatening adult, and this had been far more frightening for her than any of the stories where she had encountered monsters with gruesome masks or snakes or witches. Later in the session, the students had the opportunity to play the grumpy old man and Emma performed that role with enthusiasm.

Just to recap what was a very therapeutic process. I observed the student was alarmed and that there was something in that particular scenario that was very real for her. When Emma refused to look at me and seemed frozen to the spot I knew that we had to work with the art form to help her to stand her ground in such a situation and respond to the threat rather than freezing. I did this by giving her a trusted adult who delivered the line for her in the first instance and encouraged her to grab the sun when the old man's back was turned. She was able to do that. She mobilized herself once she had a support person and this built her confidence. I then took her one step away from the stimulus and let her watch other students confront the old man until she was ready to try again. It was important for her to role-play the old man – to be the one perceived as all-powerful and experience what it was like to interact with the fearful child.

Using stories that involve characters with whom they can identify increases your chances of getting students to engage and participate in the session. Drama is an ideal medium for the playing out of forbidden impulses, and the morally ambiguous nature of the heroes in these stories can provide fertile ground for discussion with more verbal students.

7

Stories of a Special Child

Stories of a miraculous birth are common in mythology, with the most famous being the Christian story of the birth of Jesus. In secular society, it is not uncommon for children, and not just those with an intellectual disability, to have no idea why we celebrate Christmas. When asked they often reply that Christmas is about Santa and gift giving. I am not a Christian but I think it is important that we acknowledge the origins of a major worldwide celebration. For me, it is the story of the birth of a special child, and the therapeutic aspect lies in the theme of universal rejoicing and celebration that accompanied that birth regardless of the humble beginning.

The nature of the baby Jesus' conception was miraculous, but in many ways the safe delivery of a healthy child is a miraculous occasion also which in an ideal world is greeted with great joy not only by the immediate family but also by the wider community. For many of the children with whom I work, there was no such celebration. Some were clearly disabled at birth and some needed specialist care for the first months of their lives. Some were separated from their mothers and fathers and when reunited had difficulties bonding. Some students with whom I work are not and have never been raised in their family home.

Some parents were in a position to prepare themselves for the arrival of the baby with special needs and did everything they could to welcome the child but they still had to deal with widespread ignorance and lack of acceptance of difference in other people's responses to their newborn.

A proportion of the students with whom I work suffer neglect and in some cases abuse. For some students, the neglect is more to do with socio-economic factors in their home environment than their disability. For others, the neglect occurs because of their disability, and the shame which the family feels at having a less than perfect child turns into anger and resentment towards that child. There are also many challenges involved in caring for a child with a disability and it may be that this combines with other factors to produce a system of abuse. Whatever the reasons, the schools do what they can to mitigate the effects and in some cases call in outside agencies to intervene.

This chapter addresses some of the psychological issues of being a learning disabled or profoundly disabled child. I became aware of the power of this image, the charge behind it and what Jung would call the 'numinous' dimension, not in a story of a miraculous baby but in the Native American creation myth of 'Morning Star, Evening Star'. Ostensibly a story about the birth of the planet earth, it is on some level a macrocosm of the birth of a child.

In an enactment of the story with a group of 7-year-olds with Down syndrome, I realized that the part they were most driven to play, in which they all participated and wanted to repeat, was the moment when the pebble that has been dropped into the ocean emerges as the new planet. The stars, who brought about this act of creation, sprinkled the earth with seeds and watched in wonder as trees, flowers, grasses and all manner of good things took root, grew and bloomed. While each child hid under a gauzy, iridescent black fabric and then on cue rose up in the centre of the circle with arms out-stretched to be sprinkled and marvelled at, the narrator intoned, 'Morning Star, Evening Star, Little Star and all the other stars in the sky looked down on the earth and they smiled because they saw that they had created was very fine.'

While the stories of Momotaro and Morning Star/Evening Star allow students to enact a positive birth experience, the story of Maui may more closely mirror their actual life experience. One of the functions of drama therapy is to provide the opportunity to heal from a painful experience by enacting an alternative scenario. The story of the birth of Maui describes initial rejection by the mother, subsequent nurturing by an adoptive parent, and ends with a joyful reunion with the mother and the extended family.

The birth of Maui

Maui was born early, the fifth son in his mother's old age. She thought he was dead and instead of burying him with special ceremonies as was custom, she wrapped him in her hair and threw him out to sea. However, Maui was not dead but floated safely in his cradle of hair and kelp until he was rescued by Tama-nui-te-ke-rangi, the god of the sea. Tama loved and cared for the boy teaching him how to take on the shape of birds and many magic tricks that would be unknown to his brothers. When Maui was grown, Tama drew the boy to him and said, 'You must go and find your people now, my bones are old and I'm off to see my friends in the underworld.'

Maui thanked him: 'You have been both mother and father to me. I will never forget you.' Then he set off to find his people.

He searched far and wide, over mountains and through forests and streams until one day he came to a village. He went into the meeting house where a beautiful woman was talking to her four sons. Maui recognized her immediately and felt he had come home. The woman was telling the young men to get ready for the festivities and she was counting them in order of age: 'Come Maui-mua (Maui the first) and then Maui-roto (the middle) and Maui-taha (the side) and lastly Maui-pae (the edge), that's four.'

But Maui stepped forward from the shadows and said, 'Here I am, mother.'

Taranga stared at the young boy in amazement and said, 'Who are you?'

'I am Maui, your last born son, the one you thought was dead.'

Taranga's eyes filled with tears and she said, 'Is it true? Can it be you? Yes, it is you! The baby I thought had come too soon. I will call you Maui-tikitiki-a-taranga,' which means Maui formed in the topknot of Taranga.

Then there was much rejoicing throughout the whole village and people were amazed when Maui turned himself into the kereru, the wood pigeon, and performed other magic tricks. But his brothers were not pleased for they saw how the love in their mother's eyes shone for him and that at night she shared her sleeping mat with him, enfolding him in her cloak.

Themes in the story

The story of Maui's birth explains his status as trickster demi-god who loves to cause mischief and mayhem. Taranga's failure to carry out the appropriate rites for the child is responsible for Maui's propensity for spite and mischief. The rites give the parents the opportunity to grieve the dead child as well as mollify the spirit of the child born dead. The mother was disrespectful to the 'dead' child. Although cradled in her topknot, he became flotsam and jetsam, the rubbish of the sea. Her failure to observe the appropriate rites insulted him at a very tender age.

Tama, the adopted mother/father, is a stark contrast to Taranga as he nurtures, plays with and teaches the child. He is responsible for teaching Maui the magic that will later make him such a formidable adversary. He is the grandfather figure who has the time and the patience to give to the child. It is interesting to consider here that in many Pacific island communities it is not uncommon for the grandparents to raise the child. This theme of the positive connection between the very old and the very young also occurs in the story of Momotaro (later in this chapter) where the boy found by the old couple will be 'the joy of our old age'.

The theme of the negative consequences of rites not being observed or a failure to pay respect where respect is due is common in stories from all over the world. The fairy not invited to the christening of the infant princess curses her, and the entire court is affected in the story of 'Sleeping Beauty'. In Greek mythology, Eris, or Discord, was the only god not invited to the wedding feast of Thetis and Peleus. Outraged, she threw a golden apple inscribed with the words 'to the fairest' amongst the guests and the ensuing competition between Aphrodite, Hera and Athena resulted in the Trojan War!

The story of Maui's birth contains a very powerful theme of sibling rivalry that reoccurs in all the stories of Maui and his brothers. From their perspective, Maui is the interloper with special powers who takes their mother's affection from them. I have used this story in workshops with groups of children who are siblings of a child with a disability. Another aspect of being in the family of a child with a disability is that they may be perceived to be the most important person in the family whose needs are given precedence and around whom the rhythms of the family revolve. In these cases, it is the non-disabled child whose needs are neglected or who feels usurped in the mother's affections.

Ideas for the story

In one class, the teacher had a large saucer-shaped plastic container about six feet wide filled with brightly coloured balls. The students would sit in this saucer, rock in it, and hide beneath the balls. It held positive associations for students who used it as a pleasant place to take themselves off to when they needed. I substituted polystyrene pieces from a packing case and heaped them up in the saucer. The student playing Maui got into the saucer and hid beneath the polystyrene while we dragged and rocked the saucer across the floor. All the students shrieked with glee when Tama discovered them. It was like a variation on the games of peek-a-boo or hide and seek when the child leaps out to the amazement of the adult. In another class, we used the lycra dragged on the polished floor by myself and other students and filled with shredded newspaper. For Taranga's hair, we used a number of balls of wool that we spent some time unravelling and teasing out to produce a soft, warm mat. In one class, the teacher took students down to the beach to look at the flotsam and debris and collect seaweed and driftwood in order to make a collage piece of artwork of the cradle of Maui.

'I turn you into this' is a game I devised in response to the large number of stories I used which involved transformation of one sort or another. Ovid's *Metamorphosis* is an entire collection of stories involving this theme. In this game, the student points a magic wand at another student and says or signs an animal or thing he must change himself into, or, in other words, pretend to be. Examples are pigs, chickens, birds, spiders, or other figures familiar to the class, like giants, fairies or ogres. You can remind the whole class of all the animal sounds with which they are familiar in order to get a good response to this game and, as usual, any response by the student is applauded. In one class, a student said to Justin, a student with autism, 'Turn yourself into a car' and quick as a flash the teacher aide sat down beside him miming holding a steering wheel and said, 'Come on, Justin, make the sounds,' which the student did perfectly. It just so happened that making impressive mechanical sound effects was Justin's forte. Students are delighted at their ability to make someone else change and sometimes the power involved can be quite intoxicating and they don't want to stop changing everyone into something else.

I really wanted the return of Maui to be special and to emphasize, as the story does, the image of each son having a place and Maui finding his. Therefore, I used the tune of 'Frère Jacques' for this song. This is repeated saying 'Maui in the middle, Maui on the side, Maui on the edge' for each subsequent son.

> Where is Maui, where is Maui?
> Here I am, here I am
> Maui, the first one, Maui, the first one,
> Here I am, here I am.

We laid pieces of coloured card in a V formation on the ground to identify where each student should stand with the firstborn at the front, the middle one behind him and the other two on either side. The student playing Maui calls in a loud voice from behind the others, 'Here I am, Mother,' to which she replies, 'Who are you?' In an equally loud voice, he calls out, 'It is I, Maui, your last born son.' The dialogue has similarities to the dialogue I use in the story of Maui and the sun where the sun asks from beneath the net that is imprisoning him, 'Who are you?' and Maui replies, 'It is I, Maui.' I really wanted to have students asserting themselves in the same way that Maui does with a strong sense of his own identity. Many of the students I work with have great difficulties with this in the same way that they have difficulties engaging their musculature and physical strength at will. They may be very loud and physically aggressive when angry or frustrated, but to get them to use their weight and strength to push or to use their voice to dominate a room in other than a reflexive way is difficult.

Momotaro

There once was an old couple who were very poor. They and other people in the village had had all their things of any value stolen by ogres many years before. One day the old woman was down by the edge of the river washing the laundry when she saw something bobbing in the water. As it came nearer, she realized it was a giant peach. She was very excited and called for her husband to come and help her drag it from the river. Together they got the giant peach up onto the shore and sat gazing at it in wonder. Finally, the old woman said to her husband, 'Shall we eat it?'

He replied, 'Yes, let's!' and, fetching a machete, began to cut through the fruit.

Suddenly the fruit broke in two and what do you think was inside? Where the peach stone should have been there was a lovely baby boy! The old woman cried out, 'Oh, husband, a baby! Shall we keep him?' and her husband replied, 'Yes, he will be the joy of our old age.'

So they took the baby boy home and raised him together and called him Momotaro which means son of a peach. He did indeed bring them great joy until one day when he was fifteen years old he announced to them that he was going to fight the ogres and get back all their riches. His parents were dismayed as they feared for his life, but he told them not to worry and that he was determined to go. His mother baked him millet dumplings for the journey and his father went into the forest and cut him a stout staff for walking. Then, bidding his parents goodbye, he set off.

He strode through valley and hills and walked at a good pace until he decided to stop for some refreshment. He found a nice sheltering tree to sit under, sat down and began to unpack the dumplings his mother had baked for him. Suddenly he heard a loud rustling in the bushes and a large brindled dog leapt forth with its teeth bared. 'Who are you to enter my territory unannounced? Pay homage to me or I will bite off your head!'

At this Momotaro started laughing and said, 'I am Momotaro and I am not afraid of you. Be off with you!' and he waved his staff at the dog who retreated to the bushes with his tail between his legs.

'Oh, Lord Momotaro,' said the dog, 'please accept my humble apologies and tell me what brings you to these parts.'

Momotaro gladly told him of his quest, the dog's eyes lit up and he began to wag his tail with glee. 'Oh, please let me go with you, lord, I am an able fighter and will be a faithful retainer.' Momotaro thought for a moment and then agreed. He shared his millet dumpling with the dog and then together they set off.

It was a beautiful day and they covered lots of ground before it began to get dark and they stopped to sleep in a forest under a tree. Just as they began to settle to sleep a monkey swung down from the trees and presented himself to Momotaro. 'Your reputation precedes you, Lord Momotaro,' said the monkey. 'I would be honoured if you would allow me to be your loyal retainer and accompany you to fight the ogres.'

Momotaro beamed and said, 'I can see that you will be an amusing and playful companion. Join us.' Then he shared his millet dumplings with both new friends and they settled to sleep for the night.

The next day was glorious and all three made good time as they travelled swiftly across land. Suddenly the dog raced off into the bushes pursuing a magnificent pheasant. The bird, finding itself cornered, turned and pecked at the dog, fending him off until Momotaro arrived. Momotaro exclaimed, 'What a valiant bird this is defending himself against a much fiercer animal. He would make a valuable companion in our quest. Will you join us?' The pheasant was glad to join the others and the four of them set off.

After a time, the countryside began to change. They left the green fields behind and the landscape became more barren, until finally they reached the shore and gazed out to sea. Momotaro sent the pheasant off to fly over the sea and find the island of the ogres. Meanwhile the others busied themselves constructing a boat out of bamboo stalks to sail to the island. When the pheasant returned they all set sail to the ogre's island.

They landed the raft where it could not be seen and crept to the ogres' castle. The dog bit a hole in the castle fence and he and Momotaro crept through. The pheasant flew up to the castle walls and called out, 'Ken-ken, ken-ken,' which means, 'There is an earthquake coming.' The ogres all fled through the gates and the monkey pelted them with stones, Momotaro thrust at them with his sword and the dog bit them mercilessly. The pheasant dived from the sky and blinded them with his sharp beak.

By the morning, the battle was over and Momotaro and his friends were able to return home with all the treasure which they had found in the ogres' castle. They were welcomed in triumph to the village and lived together for many years with his overjoyed parents.

Themes in the story

'Momotaro' is one of the most famous stories in Japan and it describes a child with superhero qualities. In some versions of the story, Momotaro experiences accelerated growth and is only 5 years old when he decides to go and fight the ogres although he has the strength and emotional maturity of a young man. What I do not usually include in the version I use with groups is that the ogres actually stole the children of the village, so that Momotaro, by his very presence, is healing for the old couple and the community. It also explains how fearful his parents must have been when he was so determined to confront the ogres. A familiar theme is the animal companions who have attributes that equip them uniquely for the task.

Ideas for the story

The story begins beside a river. I often sing the opening song while wafting a long length of blue fabric above the students' heads with another staff member holding the other end. You can make it a game where students can only come beneath the fabric when they are sitting nicely and each time you sing the song you point to another two students until finally the whole class is seated beneath the fabric. This activity is so popular that I often integrate it into other sessions with different songs and different coloured fabric. It makes a most calming, settling activity with which to begin the session.

> The river is flowing, flowing and growing,
> The river is flowing down to the sea.
> Carry me off with thee,
> Thy friend I will always be,
> Carry me off with thee,
> Down to the sea.

The scene with the old woman doing her washing in the river falls nicely into a sequence, which I have described in Chapter 2 (see page 31). We then sing the following song in call and response with appropriate actions.

> Washing in the river (Mime washing the laundry)
> What do we see? (Hand on brow)
> A great, big, peach (Mime a big, round shape)
> Floating down to me. (Make the shape of waves with one hand)
> Shall we have it for our dinner? (Hand on hips)
> Have it for our tea? (Rub tummy)

Shall we cut it in the middle? (Mime cutting with flat of hand)
Oh, who can this be? (Exclaim with astonished expression)

I often use a Swiss ball as the peach, which can be very satisfying to 'chop' with the side of the hand. You can have the student curled up small beside it ready to jump out as Momotaro.

This is an adaptation of 'Row, row, row, your boat' which we sing as we sail to Ogre island.

Row, row, row your boat
Gently down the stream
Merrily, merrily, merrily, merrily,
Life is but a dream.

Row, row, row your boat
Gently down the stream
If you see an ogre
Don't forget to scream.

I use masks for the animals and encourage students to provide noises for each. I often make millet dumplings with dough or playdoh, and I use a bag of scrunched up newspaper for the rocks Momotaro and the monkey throw at the ogres.

Morning Star, Evening Star

In the beginning, there were only stars. In the West dwelt Evening Star and in the East, Morning Star.

One day, Morning Star decided to visit Evening Star, so she called her sister Little Star to her and told her, 'We are going on a journey across the sky to visit Evening Star. Pack a pouch of all the things we'll need on the journey.' So Little Star packed a pouch with all things needed on a journey and then Morning Star and Little Star set off. The journey was long and the night was cold, so to keep up their spirits they sang and hummed together as they crossed the sky.

Now, far away on the other side of the sky, Evening Star saw their advance and decided to set obstacles in their path. He sent the vision of a giant cactus to impede them but Little Star just reached into her pouch and pulled out a thunderbolt, threw it at the cactus and the vision disappeared. And on the two travelled, humming and singing as they went.

Evening Star looked out across the sky and was amazed to see Morning Star and Little Star advancing towards his house. So, he decided to send another vision and this time it was of a fearsome wolf, bearing down on them slavering and howling. But Little Star just reached into her pouch and pulled out a thunderbolt, threw it at the wolf who immediately disappeared and the two carried on humming and singing as they went.

Lastly, Evening Star sent a vision of a terrible monster to menace the pair but again Little Star despatched it with a thunderbolt. Thus, Morning Star and Little Star arrived at the house of Evening Star.

Four stars guarded the house. Black Star, Yellow Star, Red Star and White Star. Morning Star confronted them and said, 'I have travelled the sky to get here and you shall obey my command. You the Black Star are autumn and you shall stand where the night begins. You the Yellow Star are spring and shall stand near the golden sun. You the Red Star are summer and shall stand in the direction of the sun. You the White Star are winter and you shall stand where the snow begins.'

The stars obeyed the command of Morning Star and they were free to enter the house of Evening Star. Then Evening Star, seeing the efforts the stars had made to see him, had a change of heart. He welcomed Morning Star and Little Star and was most gracious. Evening Star gave his power to Morning Star, Morning Star gave her power to Evening Star, and the act of creation was ready to begin.

Evening Star handed a pebble to Morning Star who dropped it into the ocean far below, and out from the ocean rose the earth. Morning Star gave some seeds to Evening Star who sprinkled them over the earth and immediately trees and flowers and all manner of greenery sprang up.

Then all the stars in the sky looked down from above on the earth and they smiled because they saw what they had created was very fine.

Themes in the story

This is a creation myth from a Native American tradition. It involves the mysterious movement of the stars and the beginning of time before the creation of the earth. There are themes of coming together and that in sharing our power with one another we can create something wonderful. In a way, this is a symbol of a positive group experience. There is the theme of creating something special out of very small and seemingly mundane things, the pebble and the seeds. There are familiar themes of an arduous journey and the overcoming of obstacles, which in reality prove a lot less overwhelming than they initially appeared. There is kinship and friendship, a sense of hope and potential. Every time I have used this story, it has been enthusiastically received. It has stimulated much discussion and interest and students have been keen to take named parts like Morning Star and Evening Star.

Ideas for the story

I was familiar with the Native American Indian concept of the beauty walk. This was a way of making sacred simple, everyday activities while honouring the earth on which we walk. I had at the time two different needs I wanted to address. One was a number of students who seemed ungrounded, who could get very 'high', and over-stimulated in drama. I saw the beauty walk as a way to focus on feet and the ground. With these students, I used laminated pieces of coloured card on which we drew students' bare feet with thick marker pens. We compared the size and shape of people's feet with one another. We then took the cards, placed them on the floor like a series of stepping stones, and asked students to step carefully from one to the other. In this way, students had to look down at their feet, bring their awareness to them, and at the same time they were literally walking in another's feet. We then practised singing the Beauty walk song while stepping, beginning with taking one step per line and then increasing it to two steps per line.

Beauty walk song

May you walk in beauty in a sacred way, may you walk in beauty each and every day.
May you walk in beauty in a sacred way, may you walk in beauty each and every day.
May the beauty of the fire lift your spirit higher. (Stretch up with straight arms)

May the beauty of the earth fill your hearts with mirth. (Bend down to touch floor)

May the beauty of the rain wash away your pain. (Hold up both hands and wriggle fingers)

May the beauty of the sky make your heart to fly. (Make a wide arc with arms in the air)

May you walk in beauty in a sacred way, may you walk in beauty each and every day.

May you walk in beauty in a sacred way, may you walk in beauty each and every day.

With one group, we were able to master the walking for the chorus, then stop for the verse, and accompany words with actions.

The other need I wanted to address was that of a profoundly disabled group who were all either in wheelchairs or on beds. Their feet were invariably encased in stout lace-up boots. I checked with both the physiotherapist and the occupational therapist that there were no physical disadvantages to removing the footwear. There were not and in fact the physiotherapist was very enthusiastic and came to support the session.

We began the session as usual with the 'Hello' song and then we all took off our shoes and staff began to very gently massage the students' feet. Because of the students' level of disability, there was virtually one-on-one staff support. For many of the students there was an immediate physical reaction to having their feet touched. Deirdre drew up in her spine and opened her eyes wide. She remained like that for several seconds until a slow smile began to spread across her features. Max, who often slept through sessions, opened his eyes and was alert for the duration of the session and for some time afterwards.

Then we sang the Beauty walk song with staff applying light pressure to the soles of the students' feet in time with the music, to give the sensation of walking. Of course, the song is also an action song which involves stretching up to the sky, bending down to the earth, making fingers into falling rain and arms stretched out to be the sky. The foot massage functioned as a warm-up to students participating in the actions of the song with the support of staff who, as they had already connected with the student, seemed to be more sensitive to their needs.

SIMPLE MIMES

There are a number of simple mimes you can do with this story. One is miming the thunderbolts. This involves putting one's hand in one's pocket and pulling out a fist, then extending the arm and opening the hand wide while making an appropriate thunderbolt sound. Similarly, when it comes to the gift giving of the stars, we mime putting our hands in our pocket and pulling out an imaginary pebble, lean over the abyss (usually some lycra), open the hand and mime dropping the pebble. Then we mime putting a hand in our pocket and pulling out some seeds and sprinkling them over the abyss. For students who need to be more concrete, we can provide real stones and seeds.

WHAT'S THE TIME, EVENING STAR?

This is a variation on the traditional children's game 'What's the time, Mister Wolf?' It involves one player standing with his back to the others who chant, 'What's the time, Evening star?' Whatever time Evening Star says becomes the number of steps the other children can take. When Evening Star says, 'Dinner time!', the children must run away before he catches someone, but when he does, the others can mime throwing thunderbolts at him to make him let the child go.

Have one student or several students go under the black fabric and emerge as a new planet. Ask them to nominate something they turn into that grows from the seeds the stars sprinkle. Some students may be able to act out their idea: a tree, an animal, or a person.

The drama sessions aim to affirm wherever possible the rightness, wholeness and integrity of each child regardless of ability. The stories in this chapter reiterate the message that how we are touched, held, spoken to, smiled and looked at in our very early stages of development profoundly influences who we will become and how we feel about who we are in our own uniqueness. Although we don't encounter students until they are at least 5 years old and often older, it is important that we praise, encourage and remind them that they are lovable even when they are as exasperating as Maui, or Jack, or the boy known as Raven.

8

Unlikely Heroes

The outcome of these stories tells the child that he who has been considered by himself or by others as least able will nonetheless surpass all. (Bettleheim, 1978, p.104)

The prevalence of the underdog theme in popular culture, in movies and on television, is an indication of its resonance with large sections of the general population; which one of us has not felt patronized or undervalued and imagined the tables being turned? It is a theme that resonates with people who are disadvantaged for a variety of reasons, those in prisons, with disabilities and mental health problems and older people. They may view themselves or be viewed by others whose job it is to help and support them, as inconsequential and incapable of making a meaningful contribution. I know that students with special educational needs who attend mainstream schools are often picked on and their disabilities mocked. A survey sent to families of children with Asperger reported an overall prevalence rate of peer victimization of 94 per cent (Little, 2002). Two of the characters in these stories are laughed at when they offer their help. Even in special schools themselves, students' abilities are often underestimated.

These stories describe how this underestimated character, the unlikely hero, triumphs with positive repercussions for the wider community. They affirm the experiences of some of the students in the group while presenting the possibility of having their true worth recognized.

There is a theme in these stories about playing to your strengths rather than your weaknesses. Everyone is different and has unique gifts that prove invaluable in certain situations with the proper supports. Yukos has good hands; the bee can identify a clever imposter by smell. It applies to the students with whom we work and their special gifts, and one of our goals as facilitators is to try to discover what they are and incorporate them into sessions. I had one student who had a wonderful singing voice. The only

115

songs she knew were songs she sang in church every week, but we found ways to incorporate them in the session and then applauded her enthusiastically.

Grandmother Spider

All the animals sit in the cold and dark talking about that wondrous element, fire, that they know people enjoy on the other side of the mountain. They decide that one of them must go and try to steal some.

The mountain lion, the king of the beasts, says he will go. He sets off over the mountain. Eventually, he sees a group of people sitting around a campfire and as he approaches, they run away screaming. However, one self-possessed individual has the presence of mind to grab a fiery brand and wave it at the lion, who is terrified and runs off. The lion returns to the camp of the animals empty-handed and dejected.

Next, the cat says she will go and she sets off over the mountain. However, when she comes across the people sitting cosily around the campfire, she is so entranced by its light and warmth that she settles down beside one of the people and falls asleep.

When the cat fails to return, the snake says he will go. He sets off over the mountain and arrives when all the people are asleep or dozing by the fire. No one notices him as he silently slithers over to the dying embers and puts down his mouth to pick up some fire. Alas, he did not realize it would be so hot and he burns his poor mouth. Fortunately, he finds a stream near by where he can hang his head in the water and cool his burned mouth. Snake returns to the animals to admit failure.

Finally, Grandmother Spider speaks up. 'Let me go,' she says, 'the people won't notice me and I have an idea of how to bring the fire back safely.' At first, everyone is highly amused that Grandmother Spider thinks she can succeed where others failed. They doubt that she can even find her way over the mountain, tiny as she is. However, she has no trouble finding her way, although it does take many days, and she spins a thread as she goes so that she can easily find her way back. When she comes to the place, no one notices her. She takes some mud and mixes it with a little saliva to form some clay that she moulds into a tiny pot, which she places carefully on her head. Then she approaches the outer reaches of the fire and finds some small embers. She moistens her fingers and quickly pops a tiny ember in her pot. Still no one notices. Then she begins her long journey back to the animals still balancing the precious pot on her head as she navigates with the help of her thread. When she arrives, the animals ask her, 'Well, did you get the fire?'

'Yes!' she says and proudly lifts down the pot to reveal the glowing ember.

The animals are amazed. They gather together brush and dry twigs and carefully lay the ember on them, gently nursing it into flame. A cheer goes up as the fire takes hold and the flames roar into life. Everyone turns to Grandmother Spider and says, 'Well, done Grandmother Spider, well done you!

Themes in the story

This story is an adaptation of a Native American Indian story that provided an explanation of how certain creatures got their distinctive features, for example the buzzard has a bald head because that is where he tried to carry the fire. It is a wonderful story, but I changed the animals to ones which I thought would be familiar to my students, the lion, the cat and the snake, and used them to try to teach ways to succeed in the achievement of a goal. The lion blunders noisily in to be easily rebuffed, the cat gets distracted from the task and the snake doesn't have enough information about the nature of what he seeks or hasn't thought enough about what to do with it once he has attained it. Grandmother Spider thinks the whole process through and returns with the fire without humans even knowing she was there. If you find a story that contains elements that you know will be attractive to your students and is full of learning opportunities do not be put off by other features that do not seem to fit. It is possible to change certain parts without losing the spirit of the story.

Ideas for the story
MAKING LITTLE POTS

I do this activity with the story of the healing waters (see Chapter 5) and it always works really well. I bring in some fresh playdoh and give a little ball to everyone. The activity can be presented as a three-stage sequence.

1. Roll the playdoh into a smooth ball.

2. Use your thumb to make a hollow in the ball to make a little pot.

3. Take the pot and place it carefully on your head.

It is good fun to see who can balance a pot on their head. To make the task more difficult I ask students to mime feeding a thread through their hands at the same time, just like Grandmother Spider. And, if they are really confident, I get them to slowly stand up and walk around with the pot on their head.

THE MAKING OF THE SPIDER WEB

This exercise has loads of learning possibilities. In its simplest form, the group sits in a circle on the floor and creates a spider web by passing a rope from one to the other and around the back of each person. Another possibility is to sit the group on chairs, pass the rope around the chair leg, and then throw it across diagonally to the next person. If it is suspended on the chair legs it is imperative no one shift their chairs around otherwise the tension goes and the web becomes slack. If you think this may be the case, throw it around staff chair legs.

Once the web shape is made, you can play around with it in various ways. You can explain or ask what the web is for (the catching of food) and that consequently the threads are sticky. The game is to leave your seat and step over the threads to reach the other side of the circle without touching any of the threads. Everyone can go 'buzzzz' if the student touches the thread and thay can chant 'chomp, chomp, chomp', which is the sound of a hungry spider coming. Encourage other students to watch closely to see if the student touches the threads.

Then you can raise the level of the web by drawing it up the chair legs and ask students to see if they can crawl under the web without touching the threads. This is a great way to practise commando crawling. Sometimes plain white rope is hard to see, so either try to get brightly coloured rope or tie bright red or yellow bits of fabric along the lengths to make it more visible.

In a profoundly disabled class, we all sat in a circle with students sitting between staff legs. I used thick, industrial type rope that went behind us. We took the rope, drew it very carefully across the palms of students so that they could feel its roughness, and encouraged some students to grip the rope. Then we threw the bale of rope across the circle to one another.

RING ON A STRING

With a class of physically very able boys, I had taken narrow rope all around the furniture in the classroom and I wanted the students to follow the rope with their hands to give them an experience of Grandmother Spider's journey. Students found the task very difficult to do, so I tried it again the following week, but this time I threaded curtain rings on the rope and each student had to take one all the way around the rope. They found this a much easier exercise to do.

To convey the experience of a journey in the dark, have one student lead the others around the room with their eyes closed. Sometimes you may need to use blindfolds as some students find it physically impossible to consciously close their eyes in this situation. If this is unsuitable, you can use a length of black fabric held over people's heads as they walk around the classroom.

MAKING THE FIRE

To the tune of 'Row, row, row your boat':

> Warm, warm, warm your hands
> Round the lovely fire
> Flickering, flickering, flickering, flickering
> See the flames grow higher.

> Warm, warm, warm your hands
> Round the lovely fire
> If you want to keep cosy
> Make sure the wood's stacked high.

I made a convincing fire out of a pile of driftwood and red feathers. As Grandmother Spider, the student carefully picks up a feather and puts it in his pot. He then has to balance the pot on his head and return to the group, where she places the pot with the feather sticking out amongst the driftwood. As each student has a turn, you get a bigger and bigger 'fire'.

To the tune of 'In the jungle':

In the darkness, the ice cold darkness
The lion said 'I'll try'
In the darkness, the ice cold darkness
The lion said 'I'll try.'

Aaaah oooh ooooh wayumamaway
Aaaah oooh ooooh wayumamaway.

Then the puss cat, the sneaky puss cat
Said 'I will find the fire'
Then the puss cat, the sneaky puss cat
Said 'I will find the fire.'

Aaaah oooh ooooh wayumamaway
Aaaah oooh ooooh wayumamaway.

Then the snake said
'While you're all in bed
I'll bring you back the fire'
Then the snake said
'While you're all in bed
I'll bring you back the fire.'

Aaaah oooh ooooh wayumamaway
Aaaah oooh ooooh wayumamaway.

Then the spider, the tiny spider
Said 'I would like to try
Because the fire's hot, I'll make a small pot
And bring you home the fire.'

Aaaah oooh ooooh wayumamaway
Aaaah oooh ooooh wayumamaway.

Yukos and the monster

There was a village by the sea that was being terrorized by a
monster called Mandabon who stole down from his lair in the
Ampawig Mountains and seized the villagers' livestock. He was

always hungry. The chief was very worried and he thought to himself, 'Chickens and pigs today, our children tomorrow.' So he decided to do something about it and this is what he did.

He announced that a young man from the village should go and kill Mandabon and in return, he could marry his beautiful daughter, Buhi. However, although many young men tried, they were unsuccessful and died in the attempt and the chief found himself in the unenviable position of losing many of the promising young men in the village and being no further forward.

Finally, a young man called Yukos approached him. Yukos was not very big and not very strong but he was clever. He made fish traps for the villagers and had very nimble fingers. The chief was surprised to see him and reminded him of all his friends who had lost their lives. 'I have thought about it a lot and I have a plan I think will work,' said Yukos. For her part, Buhi liked his look and as he was about to set off up the mountain, she gave him a scarf which she said was magical and which would protect him from harm.

He put on the scarf and began his journey taking with him a long skein of thin, strong rope. As he started to climb the Ampawig Mountains, he came to a stream where there was an old woman who was having difficulty crossing.

'Can you help me across the river, young man?' she said and Yukos immediately answered, 'Yes.' The old woman was grateful for his help and let him carry her across the rocky mountain stream. When they reached the other side she said to him, 'Yukos, you are going to fight Mandabon, aren't you?'

He replied, 'Yes.'

She said, 'He is very dangerous. But I am going to give you a magic kris which will help you,' and she gave him a long, thin knife.

'Thank you,' said Yukos and he continued on his way. Eventually he found the cave of Mandabon high up in the mountains. He was very afraid. He could hear the sounds of the monster sleeping and while he slept, Yukos worked quietly to weave a trap with rope over the entrance of the cave. When he had finished, he wrapped himself in Buhi's scarf, and stood above the entrance to the cave and called out 'Mandabon, Mandabon, wake up!'

The monster awoke and became very angry. He came charging out of the cave but became trapped in the net. His head, arms and legs were caught. Yukos took the magic kris and easily dispatched him with the knife.

He returned to the village a hero, married Buhi and became chief when the old chief died.

Themes in the story

One of the ideas that the story communicates is that an attitude of humble-ness invites assistance which the person is then open to accepting. Buhi offers the scarf without any prompting from Yukos. The giving of a protec-tive 'favour' is a common feature of traditional stories and myths as well as to knights participating in mediaeval jousts. In the Grimms' story of the twelve dancing princesses, the old soldier returning from war is approached by an old woman who tells him how to avoid the trickery of the princesses and gives him an invisibility cloak. With these 'supports' the old man succeeds where other, younger, abler men have failed and has his choice of princesses to marry.

In some stories, the help is contingent on the 'hero' responding to others' need for help. This feature often appears in the form of animals whose help later proves invaluable (see the story of Vassilisa in Chapter 10). It appears in this story as Yukos responding to the appeal for help from the old woman. Although he has the scarf and the knife, Yukos must still master his own fears and retain a cool head in order to trap and kill the monster.

Ideas for the story
MAKING A CAVE

I used a table with black fabric screening the back. The person playing Mandabon has to lie in the cave and pretend to be asleep while students very quietly weave the rope across the table legs to make a trap. If they make a sound, the monster is liable to wake up and eat them!

One experience I had doing this with a class of 6-and 7-year-olds dem-onstrated perfectly the importance of flexibility and pitching the session at the developmental level of students rather than their actual age. Most of the students were developmentally around 18–24 months of age and very challenged by the demands of being in a classroom, sitting on chairs and being discouraged from thumb sucking and other self-soothing behaviours. We had previously been playing with the monster mask, a fearsome-looking latex mask that students could pull, pinch and put in their mouths if they wanted to (a quick wipe with antiseptic wipes enabled everyone to explore the mask while reducing the risk of germs). All masks fascinated Sani – he always tracked and followed my face in a mask much more than without. No one registered any alarm at the appearance of the mask – it seemed to be a curiosity and George giggled when I put it on.

We came to the part of the story where I was lying underneath the table pretending to be the monster while the teacher was tying some rope across the table legs with the assistance of a student. Suddenly I felt Juliet wriggle under the table and cuddle up beside me. She took one of my arms to place around her, settled down and made happy crooning noises. I lifted up the mask and saw three very interested faces peering under the table. Suddenly it appeared less a monster's cave than a warm, cosy den. I rapidly changed what we were doing from the imminent dispatching of the monster to Yukos cuddling the monster in his cave and discovering that a cuddle was what the monster really needed. Each student came and had a cuddle under the table and George, who had been particularly hyperactive at the start of the session, virtually fell asleep in my arms.

I began to see the sessions as an opportunity to address the students' infantile needs – to nurture, 'mother' and support their brief forays into an exploration of the environment and back again and in this way mirror the pattern of infant development. I started using stories such as 'Goldilocks and the Three Bears' and the 'Billy Goats Gruff'. I got them out of their chairs and onto laps as much as possible and used body isolation games and songs like 'Head, shoulders, knees and toes' to increase their physical awareness. In this way, I tried to give them the safety and container I felt they needed in order to move out more confidently in the world.

SCARVES GAME

A bag of scarves is always a useful prop and depending on ability, you can either ask students to choose a scarf from the bag and wear it how they wish or play the scarf game. This has two variations. In the first version, each student takes a scarf, tucks it into the back of his waistband, and then has to walk around the room trying to take others' scarves without getting his own taken. The other version involves groups of three students who link arms.

The middle student wears the scarf at his waistband, and, as a group, they have to move around the room trying to take the other teams' scarves.

CARRYING THE OLD WOMAN

The task of carrying the old woman safely across the river places physical demands and addresses proprioception needs. On one memorable occasion, the students spent almost the whole session seeing if they could lift each other or take each other's weight. This was a very valuable exercise to use with the students who were physically strong and almost full-grown. They needed to be able to manage their strength but also to focus on what they were doing and concentrate on keeping their classmate safe. They rarely had much physical contact; in fact, one student was usually very loath to be touched by anyone. This very naturally led into an exploration of carrying and holding individuals using the whole group. We played around with different ways of carrying including a fireman's lift, which one student was able to use with another much smaller student.

For other groups, I made an 'old woman' out of a sack for the body and stockings for the arms and legs. I varied the stuffing I used in order to make her heavier or lighter, as the task was complicated by having to step across the 'river' at the same time. To make the task harder, I instructed the students holding the river (the length of blue fabric) to move it from side to side and Yukos had to try to step over without getting his feet wet. In one session, I used blocks to represent stones that the student had to step on and in another session, real stones and pebbles.

Solomon and the bee

King Solomon was relaxing in his silken hammock having an afternoon snooze in his shady summer garden when a bee flew by and accidentally stung him on the nose. Solomon was outraged and called for his servants. 'An insect has stung me on my nose! Find the culprit now!' he bellowed.

The servants went throughout the garden and commanded all the insects they could find to come and present themselves to the powerful king who was nursing a swollen, red nose. The butterflies came, the ladybirds came, the cicadas came, and the little bee came and hid at the back of the crowd. Solomon went through the crowd demanding, 'Did you sting me on my nose?' Finally, he came to the little bee who humbly admitted that it was she who had stung his nose. She said it was by mistake and that she was very young and very sorry.

'Sorry isn't good enough,' said the king. 'Give me one good reason why I should not have you punished right now.'

'Well,' said the little bee, 'perhaps I may be of service to you in the future.'

At this the king roared with laughter at the thought that a little bee could be of service to a powerful ruler like himself. 'Be off with you,' he said and the little bee flew quickly away before he had a chance to change his mind.

Now King Solomon had a very good friend and her name was the Queen of Sheba. The two loved to get together and talk and take part in friendly rivalry. On one such visit, the Queen of Sheba boasted that she had artisans in her kingdom so skilled that they could make flowers impossible to distinguish from fresh flowers. King Solomon was keen to take the test to see if he could tell which were hand made and which were real, but when he examined the bunches of flowers he found it impossible to tell.

'Well, she's caught me out this time,' he thought and was preparing to admit defeat when he heard a buzzing in his ear and a voice said, 'Watch me and see where I land.' It was the little bee. As King Solomon watched, the bee alighted on the real flowers and he was able to identify the correct bunch. The Queen of Sheba was amazed and the little bee flew off knowing she had kept her word and been of service to the most powerful king in all the land.

Themes in the story

The major theme in the story is the theme of being disadvantaged in almost every way compared to the all-powerful Solomon. The bee is young, small and inconsequential. I was attracted to this story because of what I perceived as its relevance to many students, particularly the scenario of making a mistake, being in big trouble and being too frightened to own up.

Ideas for the story

HIDING THE BEE

I used an adapted version of hide and seek with a class of boys with Asperger who seemed to get too anxious when they were the one sought. They much preferred this version. For this game I had a little stuffed bee and one person had to hide his eyes while the rest of us hid the bee somewhere in the room. While the student searched, we could call out 'hot' or 'cold' to indicate how close he was to finding it with 'hot' being very close and 'cold' being very far away.

In one class of autistic boys, the dialogue we devised for the scene where the bee accidentally stung Solomon's nose produced gales of laughter from one boy, who annoyed his teacher for weeks afterwards, repeating it. We role-played Solomon lying in his hammock being fanned by servants and the person playing the bee took the stuffed bee and pretended to sting him. Solomon roared, 'What was that?' and clutched his nose. The other students called back, 'A bee!' but Solomon ignored them, shouting, 'An insect stung me on my nose. Servants, find him!' A big red clown's nose is easily available at joke shops to convey the stung nose.

As is the case with all the stories, there are opportunities for tying in drama with art lessons and having students draw and paint all the little bugs involved. One class made paper flowers and prior to the session their teacher took them throughout the grounds of the school to identify flowers which they could pick and use in the session. It was a valuable exercise in observation and in distinguishing one group from another (flowers from shrubs, bushes and trees) and provided a wonderful real-life parallel to the discrimination used by the bee in the story.

You can have great fun using fabrics and costume jewellery to dress up both students and classroom as a sumptuous Middle Eastern court. The silky hammock is easily improvised by using the lycra.

The first sail

Ten brothers lived on the island of Woja. Their people needed a chief and each brother considered himself the best choice and was fiercely jealous of the others so the eldest, Timur, made a suggestion: 'Let us have a canoe race to decide who will be chief.' The others agreed and the route was decided. It was an arduous one from Woja to Jeh Island across the stormy Pacific so the victor would indeed be a worthy chief.

On the day of the race, the brothers lined up on the shore ready to begin, when their mother, Liktanur, came hurrying along the shore with a big bundle: 'I would like to go with you. Who will take me in his canoe?'

The brothers were dismayed. Another person in the boat would severely slow their progress and make it very difficult to paddle. Timur spoke up: 'This is a man's race, mother, and you will only slow us down.' However, the youngest boy, whose name was Jabro, offered to take her and as the others thought it would have been unlikely that he win anyway this seemed a good solution.

The race began and the other boats shot off out to the open sea. Jabro laboured in his canoe and was soon left far behind. Towards evening, a light breeze sprang up and his mother untied the bundle she had been carrying to reveal a piece of cloth and two long poles. She used these to construct a sail that immediately caught the breeze and the little boat sped off across the water without the need to paddle. Liktanur showed Jabro how to move the mast to catch the wind whatever its direction and soon the boat caught up with the others.

Timur was very angry and asked, 'Why was this offered to Jabro? I am the eldest. It rightfully belongs to me.' He was so persistent that Liktanur agreed to swap boats. Jabro was dismayed. 'Why did you do that when it was me who offered to take you in my boat?'

His mother replied, 'It seems unfair, but I have not taught Timur how to tack with the wind, so as soon as the wind changes he will slow. If you paddle as hard as you can you can win the race.' So Jabro paddled with all his might and was indeed the first to land at Jeh Island. Jabro was proclaimed chief and proved himself an able leader.

At the end of their lives the brothers and their mother were magically transformed into stars which may have been the Pleiades, or what the Maori term the Matariki.

Themes in the story

The story contains a common theme of sibling rivalry and a fight for dominance and status in the group. Although it is a Melanesian story from the Marshall Islands, the theme of filial obedience is familiar to many cultures. It is unthinkable that the mother will be left behind – one of the brothers will take her and the youngest is the likeliest option.

It looks at one stage in the story as if the youngest brother will triumph purely because he had the ostensibly bad luck to have to transport the mother. Of course, it is never that easy. Just like Yukos, who also had assistance, the deciding factor will be his own ability, persistence and endurance. What happens with the eldest brother who insists on his rights is an important lesson. One can have the right to possess the technology, but without earning the knowledge, it is useless.

Ideas for the story
PADDLING A CANOE

Paddling occurs in several of the stories. I use a broom handle as the 'paddle' and a stool on wheels as the boat. Sometimes I bring in half a dozen paddles so that students can practise at the same time. It is an excellent method for encouraging students to grip, coordinate, and move a prop from one side of the body to the other. It means that they have some appreciation of what it takes to paddle a canoe across long distances and stormy seas. First, I demonstrate how to grip the paddle, which is with both hands and the knuckles facing out. Then I demonstrate the movement from one side to the other. When I think they have the idea they can come and sit on the wheeled stool and if they paddle correctly the 'canoe' will move (i.e., I push it around). As they paddle, I make shushing sounds and ask students what the sound reminds them of. If they have worked with me a lot they usually guess it is supposed to convey the sound of the water.

The activity provides a wonderful opportunity for students to experience cause and effect. When they paddle as demonstrated, the canoe moves. When they stop, or paddle incorrectly, the canoe stops moving. In one group of very able students, we were able to use five stools at the same time and with five broom handles were able to stage a race from one end of the gym to the other. One person then had to make the journey with a classmate either sitting on the stool with him or hanging on his back to convey the added burden of the extra person.

CATCHING THE WIND

As the story progresses the 'paddle' becomes the upright part of the sail. I tie a light piece of fabric to the broom handle and the student has to hold the sail broom handle upright as we move on the stool around the room. Both activities demand a lot in terms of muscular ability, balance and trust, but with support, most students can do it and for some it is an exhilarating experience.

This story also provides opportunities to explore cause and effect in the concept of tacking with the wind. For this activity, I used a room fan. A standing one is best as it is the right height, but a smaller version will do. We set it on the moving setting so the direction of the breeze changes and the student has to hold the sail and see if he can catch the wind in order to make the sail billow.

It is always good for us to be reminded that gifts reside in the unlikeliest places. Fairytales abound with examples: the jewels in the rotten apple, the beast who is really a prince. One effect of using stories which emphasize this theme is that what we are communicating to students metaphorically is that we appreciate a person's true worth and we are not taken in by appearances. The drama sessions work to affirm this in many ways, not just in the choice of story, in applauding enthusiastically, affirming individual contributions, laughing and being playful.

9

Competitiveness

In some classes, students seem relatively unaware of each other and rarely interact or glance in one another's direction. Here the drama sessions aim to extend the students' awareness of others and to provide opportunities for interaction. In some classes, however, there is an identifiable dynamic operating: the behaviour of certain students noticeably changes when a particular student is present or absent. In classes where students are closer to the 'normal' cognitive development of their age group, behaviour surfaces which includes friendship making, bullying and favouritism. In the 5- to 8-year-old stage of child development, the ability to resolve conflict becomes crucial. The issue of sharing is paramount because in order to coordinate play two children have to balance their greediness and desire to control. Most 3-year-olds cannot share consistently enough to make reciprocal play possible, but by 5, many children have made that developmental step and learned how to share. This is an achievement they need to make in order to take part in collaborative play (Thompson, O'Neill Grace and Cohen, 2001).

While certain social skills are being mastered, the strength of emotion that accompanies other aspects of socializing challenge the cognitive and communication impairments of the student. In these cases, the stories provide metaphorical discourses that mirror the student's experience while providing opportunities for reframing the problem and exploring multiple realities.

Tarantula and Swift Runner

There were once two friends who played together all the time. Their names were Tarantula and Swift Runner. Tarantula had many good qualities. He was an excellent hunter. Swift Runner was a very fast runner. After a time Tarantula began to think people did not like him while everyone loved Swift Runner. He became very jealous of his friend. He started to think that everyone loved Swift Runner because of his colourful feather headdress and his rainbow shawl. He decided to try to take the headdress and the shawl even though he knew Swift Runner loved them. One day he approached Swift Runner saying slyly, 'Swift Runner, you look so handsome in your feather headdress and your rainbow shawl but you don't know what they look like, do you? Why don't I try them on and you can see what I look like in them?'

Swift Runner innocently agreed and handed over the precious items to Tarantula who grabbed them and raced off to his burrow. He disappeared into the intersecting tunnels of the burrow where Swift Runner could not follow him.

Swift Runner was devastated, not just by the theft of his things but by the betrayal by his friend. He paced up and down outside the burrow calling for his friend to come out, but Tarantula did not listen. Finally, Swift Runner went to the gods to ask for their help. They conferred amongst themselves and then said, 'If you cannot confront Tarantula in his burrow we must tempt him to come out.'

They knew Tarantula could not resist the hunt so they took magic clay and fashioned a deer and breathed life into it and set it in front of the entrance to Tarantula's burrow. Then Swift Runner and some of his friends hid in the undergrowth and waited. Tarantula smelt the deer and crept out to the entrance to his burrow. He took his bow and arrow and began to stalk the deer. He took aim and let fly an arrow but as it hit the deer, the deer magically disappeared and Tarantula found himself on open ground surrounded by a group of his friends.

Swift Runner demanded back his things. He was very angry at Tarantula. He said, 'Why did you trick me and steal my things? I thought you were my friend.'

At this Tarantula's face fell and he admitted that he had been thinking that everyone loved Swift Runner more and that if he had a feathered headdress and a rainbow shawl they might love him too. Swift Runner forgot his anger. He forgave his friend. He hugged him and told him he could borrow his things any time he wanted.

Themes in the story

A major theme in the story is one of jealousy and rivalry. This theme occurs elsewhere, in the stories of the birth of Maui (Chapter 7) and 'The first sail' (Chapter 8). I was prompted to choose this story in the first instance by a conversation with the teacher of a satellite class of 8-year-olds. Satellite class refers to a class from a special school based at a mainstream school.

A new student, Jason, arrived in the class who was extremely sociable and well behaved. He received a great deal of positive affirmation from his teacher, visitors to the school and other children in the class. What was more, he was able to play with the other children from the mainstream school to which the class was attached.

Another student, Simon, was always getting into fights with other children in the mainstream school and was often shunned. However, he desperately wanted to be a part of one particular group of children, but did not have the social skills to gain entry. Simon was a student who had an invisible disability. He had been born prematurely, at a low birth weight and not expected to survive. Instead, after a worrying period in intensive care he had gone on to thrive and reach some developmental milestones at the appropriate age. However, his prematurity affected his brain in such a way that he had very low impulse control and a higher propensity to aggression. He was a risk taker unable to navigate roads on his own due to his complete lack of road sense. Because in many ways he was higher functioning than his classmates, Simon longed to distance himself from them and ally with students in the mainstream. His failure to do so was no doubt exacerbated by the arrival of Jason, who although cognitively not as bright as Simon, was socially very competent.

Simon quickly developed a visible antipathy towards the new student. He began by being verbally abusive, quietly muttering under his breath in class, and then started to target Jason in playground games where he would 'accidentally' bowl him over. Up until now, Jason appeared relatively unaware he was being singled out by Simon for unfair treatment.

In the enactment of the story, Simon was initially attracted to the role of Swift Runner because he said he was a fast runner, 'the fastest in the class'. Nevertheless, he changed his mind and opted to play Tarantula, partly, I think, because of the opportunity to play a trick, which was something he loved doing. Some drama therapists might say that he was unconsciously choosing the scenario with which he most closely identified. In the role of Tarantula, Simon experienced in a compressed timeframe and contained environment what the consequences of his actions were. Tarantula obtained the headdress and the shawl but was isolated by his action. It was a very hollow victory, and short lived, as he himself was then tricked into coming out into the open and being confronted by Swift Runner with the support of others.

After this enactment, I initiated a discussion with the class around the word 'jealousy'. Simon was one of the few students able to tell me what the word meant. He said, 'It's when you want something the other person has.'

I said, 'That's right, and what does Tarantula want that Swift Runner has?'

Jocelyn said, 'He wanted those,' and indicated the shawl and headdress.

At this point, the teacher intervened to speak to Simon directly. She said, 'Do you think he *really* wants the shawl and the headdress?'

Simon said, 'No, he wants people to like him.'

This response indicated the extent of Simon's cognitive understanding of the story and the process of enacting had enabled him to have a felt understanding also.

The teacher continued, 'Do people like him more when he has the shawl and the headdress?'

Someone else in the class answered, 'No.'

Some of the students looked as if they were losing concentration at this point so I organized another enactment, this time with Simon as Swift Runner. When it came to the part where he realized he had been tricked, Simon went to the others with his palms upturned and began to speak without any prompting from me. 'Please, can you help me, he's taken my stuff and I can't get them back.'

When Tarantula came out of his burrow, three other students went with Simon to talk to him. I froze the action at this point to ask Simon what it felt like to have the others standing behind him. He said, 'Good, he's [Tarantula] going to listen to me now.'

After this enactment, we had a further general discussion about the themes in the story. After all, Simon was not the only student in the class to have issues around jealousy and competitiveness and feeling unloved. I asked them, 'Is there anyone in the class who you think is a bit like Swift Runner in that everyone seems to like them?'

Two people said 'Jason' and Jason beamed. Simon didn't say anything but he was looking very intently at me.

I said, 'Is there anyone who feels a bit like Tarantula, that nobody likes them?'

Simon said, 'I do sometimes when no one wants to play with me.'

His teacher asked gently, 'People in this class don't want to play with you?' and Simon hesitated and said 'No.'

Jason said, 'I'll play with you' which was followed by a chorus of other voices. Simon looked pleased.

Now this is not to say that the problem was instantly solved, but at least it had been raised and the story gave the teacher a frame of reference to address future problems as they arose. She would ask Simon, 'Are you feeling like Tarantula?' or 'How would Swift Runner deal with this situation?' whereas previously talking to Simon about his bullying or jealousy had made him feel ashamed and not in control of his own behaviour. The metaphorical nature of story may give the student just the distance he needs in order to approach the problem afresh and with less emotional charge.

Ideas for the story

The game 'Duck, duck, goose' can work really well with this story. The group sits in a circle with one less chair than there are players. The person without the chair walks around the back of the circle touching each player in turn saying, 'Duck'. When he gets to the third person, he shouts, 'Goose!' The person touched needs to leap out of his chair and chase after the first person to try to touch him before he steals his seat. If he manages to do that, the first person has to sit in the duck pond in the centre of the circle until the next player successfully catching the 'goose' redeems him. If he cannot catch the first person, he then has a turn at going around the circle saying, 'Duck, duck, goose.' In some groups, you may want to identify the person to be 'goosed' so that they can prepare to run. In this way, the game also becomes a great way to practise counting.

As this is a Native American story and involves a feathered headdress it seemed appropriate to include a set of bows and arrows in the props. Bows and arrows are relatively easy to buy but their use is often limited to students whose fine motor skills are up to the task of fitting the arrow onto a string, holding and releasing it. Interestingly, fine motor skills may be an attribute you were unaware a student had up until this point, as was the case with Hine. She was a student with a lot of language delay and cognitive impairments. However, when I gave her the bow and arrow she easily mastered it after seeing me model it only once. Some students made it obvious that they had played with a bow and arrow before so the exercise was a great opportunity to show off a skill nobody knew they had. This is why it is important not to make assumptions about a specific student's ability in an unknown area. I have often been pleasantly surprised.

This story gives really good opportunities for dressing up in the rainbow shawl (I used a length of sari material) and feathered headdress (usually available from toyshops). I used playdoh to fashion little animal figures and the tube made a good burrow for Tarantula.

Atalanta and the golden apples

Atalanta was a fine athlete and exceptional huntress. When she became a young woman, her father consulted the oracle at Delphi to divine her future and was told, 'If she marries, she will be ruined.' She decided to stay single, but many young men wished to marry her so eventually she agreed to marry whomever could beat her in a race. The losers would die and as Atalanta was such a good runner, many young men lost their lives.

There was one young man, Hippomenes, who longed to marry her and whom Atalanta herself loved. He sought the advice of Aphrodite, the goddess of love, who gave him three golden apples to distract Atalanta in the race. She also told him to pay respects to her after he had won the race. The race began and Atalanta easily pulled ahead. So Hippomenes threw the first golden apple in her path, she stopped to pick it up thus giving him the advantage, and he took the lead. Before long they were running neck and neck and realizing she was about to overtake him, Hippomenes threw down the second golden apple which Atalanta again stopped to retrieve. Hippomenes again gained the lead. Almost at the finish line, Atalanta threatened to win by a small margin, but Hippomenes threw down the last golden apple and won the race by a whisker.

The two were married and spent a blissful wedding night roaming the forests and woody hillsides that Atalanta loved. However, Hippomenes forgot to pay the tribute demanded of him by Aphrodite and as a punishment, she changed the couple into lions in danger from hunters, which Atalanta had once been herself.

Themes in the story

> One problem can arise in competitive games with the child with
> Aspergers syndrome always wanting to be first. This may not be due
> to a desire to be superior but to have consistency in the order of
> participants, to know their position and personal satisfaction in
> success. (Atwood, 1998, p.38)

With many students, the competitive element is one that makes the session
fun, but with some students, it is too much for them to handle. One such
student was Alan, a young 6-year-old boy with Asperger syndrome who
adored drama and sat on the edge of his seat with excitement as the session
started. Alan found it very, very hard to lose at anything, but even I was taken
aback at the violence of his response to the race in this story. Alan listened to
the story and knew that the young man, Hippomenes, used the apples to
distract the girl so that he could win the race. When we came to run the race,
I asked him who he wanted to be and he replied Atalanta. I reminded him
that Atalanta needs to lose the race against Hippomenes and he nodded.
Everything went according to the story, Alan as Atalanta picking up the
apples as we ran the race. However, when I, as Hippomenes, won, he was
outraged and threw a major tantrum. With tears running down his cheeks he
repeated, 'But you tricked me, you tricked me!'
  I said, 'I know, that's the only way I could win and marry you.'
  I was on the horns of a dilemma I had not anticipated. I felt it was wrong
to change the story to placate Alan because that would amount to saying
'Alright, Alan, Atalanta won that race, Hippomenes lost and so he lost his
life.' All we could do at that time was to move on as quickly as possible and
make a point of reducing the competitive element in the subsequent sessions
until his teacher thought that Alan could tolerate the possibility of losing. It
is not as if it was the presence of trickery that so upset him as Alan had loved
enacting roles in other stories where he had been the trickster. It was more
when a trick did him out of his opportunity to win. 'Other children are
determined to bend or break the rules, but the child with Aspergers
syndrome is intent on enforcing them' (Attwood, 1998, p.32).
  The story mirrors the intensity of feeling that often accompanies losing
by making the consequences life threatening. Often in sessions we are constantly reminding students that 'it is only a game' because we are trying to
help them get some perspective. This is both an adult and rational response
whereas the story metaphorically affirms the feeling of the Asperger
syndrome child, which is that losing is a life and death scenario.

There is the theme of disaster occurring with the failure to observe certain rites (see the story of the birth of Maui, Chapter 7). Hippomenes' failure to pay due respect to Aphrodite resulted in him and Atalanta being transformed into lions and unwittingly fulfilling the oracle's prophecy.

Ideas for the story

In the year 2004 the Olympic Games were held in Athens and I was asked try and incorporate the Olympic theme into sessions. I looked for a number of Greek myths and ones that involved physical prowess. The story of Atalanta seemed an ideal choice. Some teachers wanted students to have the opportunity to take part in games and had made medals and flags from the various nations taking part.

Choosing physical activities was a challenge as they had to be appropriate for students with disabilities, but after raiding the physiotherapy cupboard I had a few that worked well and were easily integrated into the Atalanta story. These included using a punch bag and boxing gloves with some of the older students, the bow and arrow, lining up weighted bottles and throwing hacky sacks at them, climbing the rope or maintaining balance to walk along the rope.

I had a brightly coloured children's toy that consisted of a small hoop about 10 centimetres wide placed on a hand-held device. You held the device and when you pulled the ripcord, the hoop spun off and glided around the room. Most students were fascinated by the leisurely glide of the hoop and would track and follow its progress. In one class of older students with autism, Erika, who was usually very reluctant to touch anything or participate in any way, reached up her index finger and placed it in the loop of the ripcord of her own accord. Together we pulled and she laughed delightedly when the hoop took off and sailed around the room. It was in Erika's class that I always included a sensory component relating to taste. The Atalanta story gave the opportunity to bring in apples, hummus, taramasalata, olives and halva (a Middle Eastern sweetmeat).

ORANGES AND LEMONS

The young men who failed to beat Atalanta in the race lost their lives and 'Oranges and Lemons' is a fun, ritualized way of acknowledging what a high price they paid and how high the stakes were for Hippomenes.

Two people make an arch out of their arms that the others go under while we sing the rhyme. On 'chop off your head', they bring their arms down and catch whoever is going under at the time. That person then joins up with the 'choppers' by putting their arms around their waists and the game continues until everyone has had their head chopped off.

'Oranges and lemons', say the bells of St Clement's.
'You owe me five farthings,' say the bells of St Martin's.
'When will you pay me?' say the bells of Old Bailey.
'When I am rich,' say the bells of Shoreditch.
'When will that be?' say the bells of Stepney.
'Of that I don't know,' says the great bell of Bow.
Bring me a candle to light me to bed
And bring me a chopper to chop off your head.

Paikea

Paikea is the story of two brothers who both want to be chief. The elder brother, Rahutapu, devises a plan to kill his brother. He carves a beautiful waka (canoe) and invites him to go out to sea with him. Once they are in the open sea, Rahutapu removes the bung from the waka and the boat begins to sink. The younger brother is struggling in the water. He chants a karakia or magic spell to give him the strength to survive. He is almost drowning when help comes in the form of a huge whale who carries him on his back to safety.

Themes in the story

The story of Paikea was the inspiration for Witi Ihimaera's 1987 novel, *The Whale Rider* which formed the basis of the 2003 film. It appears in many versions throughout Polynesia. This book includes a number of Maori and Pacific island myths as I live in New Zealand and the majority of the students I work with have a Maori or Pacific island background. I think it is important to include stories from the culture of the people with whom you are working. At the same time, using stories from the geographical area where you live provides features familiar to students regardless of ethnic background, which is also important. Using stories from other cultures is an important way of teaching students about diversity, but do not overlook the richness in the culture of the country in which you reside.

One main theme in the story is the murderous rage of one brother towards another. It demonstrates clearly that rage is blind in that in creating this wonderful waka to destroy his brother, Rahutapu brings about his own destruction. With more cognitively able groups, this story can be used to explore sibling rivalry in a similar way to Tarantula and Swift Runner as described above.

The story contains a theme similar to that in Chapter 10 of assistance arriving at the point when the hero is at his lowest ebb.

Ideas for the story
BUILDING THE WAKA

The waka is a long boat and we were able to construct one easily out of a wooden frame mounted on castors and covered with thick cardboard decorated with traditional Maori designs. We then placed a wheeled stool inside for a student to sit on, gave him a paddle and pushed from behind.

FALLING OUT OF THE BOAT

Some people may think it odd that I practise controlled falling with physically unstable students for whom falls are a common occurrence. However, the controlled element makes it an experience that can increase confidence and feelings of trust. For the boat, I use a wobble board borrowed from an occupational therapist. This is a wooden board set on curved pieces of wood so that it rocks. I am lucky enough to have access to two. One is about a metre square with handles on the top side that the student can hold on to to help maintain his balance. It is small enough for me to carry around which is a huge advantage. There is room for only one person on it but I can easily rock and then upend a smaller student on it. The second one is a lot more cumbersome as it is so much bigger and heavier. The advantage is that I can sit on it, holding the student sat in front of me before we 'fall' together.

As with many of the activities, we build in structure to increase dramatic effect and feelings of safety. I always demonstrate first and get the students to practise the scream that should accompany the fall. I sit on the wobble board, start to rock, and then begin a count of 'one–two–three' while looking very alarmed. On the count of 'three', I mime falling off the board into the 'water' with a big scream. Invariably, students scream with laughter and are usually very keen to have a go. They sit on the board and hold on to the handles while I rock the 'boat' with one big rock at the end that tips them off. They soon learn to anticipate the fall and count along too.

In a group of students with physical disabilities, one student was very agitated at the beginning of the session. She was crying and hitting herself. We simply sat together on the 'boat' with her relaxing against me and support staff rocked the board for us. We sang boat-related songs ('Row, row, row your boat'; 'Sloop John B' by the Beach Boys) and did not even attempt the fall. She calmed down quickly and stopped crying.

THE WHALE

I used the type of inflatable whale used in swimming pools and it proved to be enormously strong. I got students to sit astride the whale then lean forward so that their body was in contact with the whale (rather than sit as if astride a horse). I then bounced the whale up and down.

THE KARAKIA

In one class, the teacher spent time writing the magic song with students. Here are some examples.

Help.
The wind and sea
Will be the end
Of me.
Come,
Take my hand
Out on the sand
I'd like to be.
Watch out Paikea
Your brother's nasty
Help is out there if you ask
Hold on tight, the water's cold
Take a breath and hold.

The speech and language therapist in one school used flash cards and visuals to devise this beautiful karakia with profoundly disabled students.

Seagulls, seaweed, water, sky.
Seagulls, seaweed, water, sky.
Boy, brother

Going under
Spit and sea flows under me
Angry brother, friendly whale
Hang on tight
We're going home.
Seagulls, seaweed, water, sky.
Seagulls, seaweed, water, sky.

The more that sessions can be linked to other parts of the curriculum and the work of other members of the multi-disciplinary team, the better. When a story captures the imagination of staff as well as students, as in the example of the karakia and the speech and language therapist, there can arise a unique collaboration of people with different skills and enthusiasms that can snowball into full-scale productions or remain low key. Whatever the result, it is an extremely beneficial and creative process for students.

10

Trust

> The general state of trust, furthermore, implies not only that one has
> learned to rely on the sameness and continuity of the outer
> providers, but also that one may trust oneself and the capacity of
> one's own organs to cope with urges. (Erikson, 1995, p.222)

The issue of trust is fundamental to a person's emotional growth. In
Erikson's eight stages of personality development, basic trust versus basic
mistrust is the first pair of polarities the infant has to resolve before he can
move on. An atmosphere of trust is crucial for a group to operate therapeutically and students need to trust their teachers in order to learn. We provide an
atmosphere of trust in the drama therapy session with plentiful applause,
verbal and physical encouragement and the bringing to awareness and wit-
nessing of individual strengths. In special education, we have support staff
whose job it is to support students to learn. They are entrusted with a wide
range of duties from helping a student to eat or go to the toilet, to sitting
with a student helping them to read.

The heroes of these three stories have to trust in their inner and external
supports in the face of sometimes overwhelming obstacles. In the six-stage
story structure outlined in Chapter 2, we see that adequate supports are
crucial to the successful attainment of any goal. Each story has its own distinctive way of looking at the attainment of a goal and offers students
different perspectives. Psyche's supports come from unexpected sources.
Against the power and ire of a goddess, Psyche needs all the help she can get.
The first support comes in the form of very minute creatures whose strength
lie in their numbers and ability to work together, another familiar theme.
Psyche accomplished the second task by avoiding confronting the danger
head-on, and instead, applying patience and stealth to take what was needed
indirectly, another familiar theme as we can see in the story of Kahakura.

In the third task, she has to trust the eagle to perform the task for her. In
the story of Vassilisa, the solution to the problem lies in resting after a period

of effort and to momentarily stop focusing on the goal. There have been numerous examples from the history of science and mathematics where breakthroughs have occurred while resting after a period of intense concentration on the problem to be solved. Vassilisa has to trust the advice of the little doll, her dead mother's representative, whose love continues to sustain and protect her from harm. Kahakura has trust that the answer will come and faith in the messages he receives from his unconscious.

Psyche and Amor

A mortal woman, Psyche has fallen in love with the god Amor and he with her. The problem is his mother Aphrodite who is violently opposed to the match. When Psyche throws herself on her mother-in-law's mercy, Aphrodite takes the opportunity to set her three tasks which she must do or never see Amor again.

Aphrodite takes Psyche to a grain barn where sacks and sacks of grains and beans lie mixed up on the floor. She orders her to sort the grain into sacks. Psyche tries but it is a monumental task and she falls into despair. The ants come to her rescue. They come out of the woodwork and millions of them work to sort the grain into piles ready for Aphrodite's inspection. Aphrodite is convinced someone has helped Psyche and she is very displeased.

So she takes the girl to a grove by a stream where golden sheep and rams wander and commands her to fetch some golden fleece. The rams are too fierce for Psyche to approach them and steal the fleece. Unable to do the task, Psyche goes to the stream to throw herself in, but a reed stops her and gives her some advice. It tells her not to lose heart but to wait until the heat of the sun has passed and the sheep become sleepy and docile, then to gather the wool that is snared by the briar bushes as the sheep pass by on their way to drink from the stream. This Psyche does and she presents the wool to Aphrodite who demands to know who has helped her.

The final task involves Psyche getting water from the river Styx at its most treacherous point where it is guarded by dragons. Of course, for Psyche it is an impossible task and she again despairs but help this time comes in the form of an eagle who sails down from the sky, plucks the cup from her fingers, flies over the dragons and dips the cup into the ice-cold waters, returning with the precious contents.

After Aphrodite sees that she has completed this task, she realizes that Psyche is a worthy wife for her son and reluctantly agrees to reunite her with her husband. There follow great celebrations amongst the gods and the couple live happily ever after.

Themes in the story

This story is a simplified version of the original Greek story which included an additional task that Psyche had to perform: a hazardous trip to the underworld. I wanted to keep the symmetry of the three tasks and the fourth is a complex task, sufficient for a story in itself, which although Psyche fails to complete successfully, nevertheless results in her being reunited with her lover. From the outset, Psyche is overwhelmed by the difficulty of the tasks. Her despair clearly demonstrates the danger of goals made impossible to attain because of lack of support. It also demonstrates that sometimes help is only available when we are at the point of giving up. The story communicates a very clear message that we need to trust that this is going to happen.

Ideas for the story

I was intrigued by the image of the sorting of the grain as I had students whom I knew would be very meticulous in the carrying out of this task. I filled a bag full of chickpeas, kidney beans and black-eyed beans which I thought would be relatively simple to distinguish from one another. Sure enough, when I emptied the bag of beans onto the floor there was one student who was absorbed in the task of sorting them long after the others had lost interest!

Obtaining the golden fleece from the grumpy rams became a stealth game with cotton wool spray-painted gold sellotaped onto a staff member's back. Students had to creep up on the 'ram' without being butted.

'Bullrush' or 'British bulldog' was a good way for students to experience being up against the odds and metaphorically play at trying to get the water from the Styx without being eaten by dragons. It is a game best played in a large space. The object of the game is to get across to the other side of the room without being tagged. It begins with one player in the centre trying to catch players as they run across. Whoever is caught joins the first player in trying to catch others. Finally, there are only one or two players left who have to run across without being caught by larger numbers of players.

We had great fun in a class full of boys dressing up as Aphrodite with a long curly blonde wig and lots of gold jewellery. I explained that in Greek theatre all the parts were played by men and boys and they seemed to really enjoy the opportunity to play a 'goddess' and an imperious one at that!

Vassilisa and Baba Yaga Bony Legs

Once there was a blacksmith and his wife who had a lovely daughter named Vassilisa. When she was still young, her mother became sick. Knowing that she was dying, she called Vassilisa to her and gave her a little doll saying, 'Whenever you need help, feed the little doll and ask her what you should do.' Soon after this, the mother died.

The blacksmith remarried. He chose a widow with two daughters of her own because he thought that she would be kind to Vassilisa, but the widow had used up all her love on her own daughters and had none left over for poor Vassilisa. Besides, Vassilisa was very fair and much loved in the village and the woman was jealous, as her two daughters were very plain. The three of them made Vassilisa's life difficult, insisting that she do all the dirtiest chores and sending her out in all weathers in the hope that the wind and rain would ruin her good looks. However, no matter what they did, Vassilisa continued to grow more beautiful and the daughters became uglier with pinched bitter faces.

Then one day the blacksmith gathered his family together and told them, 'I have work in the court of the Tsar and I must go to Moscow. I will be gone for some time.' He said to his wife, 'Look after my Vassilisa till I return,' for, you see, he had no idea of her cruelty.

As soon as he was gone, the three women started plotting and they soon came up with a plan. They let the fire go out in the grate and all the candles burn down and then they said to Vassilisa, 'You must go into the forest, to the house of Baba Yaga and find fire or we will all perish with the cold.'

Obediently, Vassilisa set out into the forest. It was cold and dark already and she was most afraid. She took out her little doll, gave it a crumb from her pocket, and said, 'What will become of me?'

'Do not fear, Vassilisa,' said the doll 'follow the path through the forest and all will be well.'

Soon the path came to a clearing and before Vassilisa was an incredible sight: a house that stood on chicken legs and paced around inside a fence made up entirely of human bones with human skulls with lights inside atop of them. It was the house of Baba Yaga Bony Legs.

Vassilisa followed the path to the magic gate that opened to admit her and a head peered out of the window – a fearsome sight – a woman with iron teeth and a long hooked nose. She cackled as she watched Vassilisa approach and called out, 'Welcome, my pretty one, come in, come in!'

Vassilisa entered the house of Baba Yaga and straightway was attacked by a bird that swooped down from the rafters.

'Leave her, Voronooska,' said the witch 'she is our guest.'

As she came towards the fire, a cat bared its claws at her and hissed.

'Leave her, Grumble Guts,' said the witch 'she is our guest.'

Inside the room sat a bear with many teeth who growled at her.

'Leave her, Misher Masher,' said the witch 'she is our guest.'

Then she turned to Vassilisa with a gruesome smile and said, 'What can we do for you, my pretty one?'

'Please, Granny,' said Vassilisa politely, 'my stepmother has sent me for a light.'

Baba Yaga sat her down in front of a loom and said to her, 'Do a task for me and maybe I'll give you a light, but should you fail, I will eat you.'

Vassilisa trembled as Baba Yaga told her to spin 100 yards of silver cloth before dawn and with that, she swept off to fly through the sky in her mortar and pestle.

As soon as she was gone, Vassilisa put her head in her hands. She knew there was no way she could fulfil the task and Voronooska, Grumble Guts and Misher Masher would make sure she could not escape.

Suddenly she remembered her little doll. Taking it from her pocket, she gave it a crumb and asked it for help. 'Do not worry, Vassilisa, all will be well. Rest awhile,' said the doll.

Vassilisa closed her eyes gratefully for she was very tired. She slept soundly and awoke with a start at first light. She heard the sounds of Baba Yaga returning and anxiously looked around the room. To her relief, there on the windowsill was 100 yards of the most beautiful silver cloth. Baba Yaga swept into the room and spying the cloth, she gnashed her teeth in rage for she had been looking forward to eating the girl.

'So, you managed to complete the task, my pretty, but your travails are not yet over. Weave me 100 yards of golden cloth by the time I return or I will surely eat you.'

And with that, Baba Yaga flew off in her mortar and pestle leaving Vassilisa disconsolate.

Suddenly she remembered the doll. Reaching in her pocket, she fed a crumb or two to the little doll and then told it her plight. 'Never fear, Vassilisa, all will be well. Rest awhile and I will sort it out.'

Vassilisa was woken by the sound of the witch returning. She looked about her fearfully, but relaxed when she caught sight of the 100 yards of golden cloth sitting atop the sill. Baba Yaga was not happy when she saw the cloth. 'So, you have completed the task, but I am not ready to give you fire till you have done one more final task. Weave me 100 yards of diamond encrusted cloth before I return or I shall eat you.' With a gnash of her iron teeth Baba Yaga sped off.

Immediately, Vassilisa consulted her doll who told her to rest and all would be well. Sure enough on Baba Yaga's return, there on the sill was 100 yards of diamond-encrusted cloth. Baba Yaga was furious. 'Well, I'm going to eat you anyway,' said the witch and she went out of the back of the house to fetch firewood to stoke up the oven.

While she was gone, Vassilisa appealed to her little doll. 'Little doll, help, BabaYaga is going to eat me,' said the girl.

'Let's go and have a look and see what's in the pantry,' said the doll. They went to look and the pantry was pathetically bare.

'What are we going to do now?' wailed Vassilisa in a panic.

'Look a little closer,' said the doll. Sure enough, what Vassilisa had thought were twigs turned out to be fish and what she thought was a stone was a collection of pies, cakes, and all manner of good things.

'Give the fish to the cat,' said the doll. When Vassilisa did this the screeching cat turned into a content little puss with a loud purr.

'Give some of the pies and cakes to the bird and the bear,' said the doll.

Vassilisa did this, the bear rolled over to get his tummy rubbed, and the bird sat on her shoulder and began to rub his beak gently against Vassilisa's face.

'Quick!' said the doll, 'Now's your chance.'

Vassilisa ran out of the house and down the path where she came to the magic gate that, of course, remained steadfastly shut.

'Oh no,' cried Vassilisa, 'food will not persuade this gate to open. What shall we do?' With that, she began to cry and her tears fell on the hinges of the gate that creaked open leaving her way clear to escape. She grabbed one of the skull lamps as she left and ran through the forest all the way home.

When Baba Yaga returned with the firewood to find her gone, she was furious. 'Voronooska, Grumble Guts, Misher Masher, why did you let her escape?' cried the witch.

'Because she gave us good things to eat and you never give us anything,' replied the three.

Meanwhile, as Vassilisa approached her home, her stepmother and stepsisters were looking out the window when they saw what they thought was a disembodied skull hurtling towards the house from the forest. They immediately took fright and ran screaming from the house never to be seen again.

Vassilisa entered her home, took the lamp, lit a fire in the grate and all the candles around the house, and lived there very contentedly until her father returned from the court of the Tsar. She told him her story and he was very sorry that she had suffered so much at the hands of the woman he had married.

And the two of them lived happily ever after.

Themes in the story

The beginning of the story has similarities with Cinderella in the death of the mother, father's remarriage and the heroine's cruel treatment at the hands of a spiteful stepmother and stepsisters. There is a theme of making your enemies your allies when the story describes how to turn seeming obstacles into supports, if you deal with them in the right way. It conveys in story form a good psychological understanding for students to have, which is that underlying most aggression is either fear or a need that is not being addressed. When Vassilisa feeds Baba Yaga's animals, she turns them into friends. This situation also occurred spontaneously in the session described on pages 121–2 when I changed the story from one involving killing the monster to one involving cuddling the monster and making friends with it.

When Vassilisa weeps on the gate she has reached a similar place to Psyche in the previous story in that she knows that the strategies she has been using hitherto will be worthless in this instance. That very despair opens the gate to her freedom. It mirrors Rapunzel restoring her lover's sight and Beauty reviving the beast in the classic fairy tales.

Ideas for the story

This story includes some dialogue and is structurally more complex than a number of other stories in this book. I have used it in groups of students who had some verbal skills and the cognitive ability to remember cues. With one group, I worked in collaboration with the speech and language therapist to make the story into a short play which we rehearsed and performed in front of the school at assembly. A proviso I always make with work which involves a performance is to remember that the process component is always the most important. Try not to focus on the quality of the performance, but on the quality of the experience for the individual student and the group.

Remember the phrase 'anyone who wants a turn, gets a turn' so that if three students want to play one role, find a way of enabling them to do that. The main thing is to have fun and build confidence.

Kahakura

In the old days, the men would go out in small boats close to shore and fish the plentiful fish with a line, but it was a very time-consuming occupation and no matter how hard the men worked there was never enough fish for everyone in the village and often people would retire to bed hungry. At that time, Kahakura was chief of the village and he would spend hours thinking of a better way to fish, to no avail. Sometimes others in the village would grumble when they saw Kahakura sitting gazing out to sea deep in thought; some even accused him of laziness but Kahakura knew that what he was doing was very important for the life of the village.

So much was the problem on his mind that he would often dream about it and one night he had a very vivid dream. He dreamed of a long white sandy beach and he knew what he found on that beach would provide an answer to the problems that beset the village. When, the next morning, he told the rest of the villagers that he planned to go on a journey to find the long white sandy beach some were frankly sceptical. However, he set off at sunup and tramped across the island in the direction he felt impelled to go. He cut through bush and waded streams and climbed rocks and finally, just as the sun was going down, he pushed through a huge clump of toi toi and there in the light of the setting sun he came upon the long white sandy beach of his dreams.

The sun set and the moon rose and Kahakura realized that the beach was not empty as he had first thought. Quickly, he took cover and watched to see who the strangers were. How amazed he was to see a tribe of fairy folk wading thigh high into the water and fishing with something Kahakura had never seen before. It was a series of thin ropes knotted together this way and that way to make a cunning device that sieved out all the water while keeping the fish.

Kahakura could immediately see the possibilities of using such a device, which was of course a net. Two men could easily catch large quantities of fish, much more than with a single line. He knew he had to get hold of one of those nets but how? Fairy folk were notoriously wary of men. However, he also knew that fairy folk were terrified of sunlight and if he could just delay them there might be a way of taking the net.

Kahakura made his way quietly down to the shore where the men were fishing and groups were taking the catch and threading them on a line through the gills for easier transportation. Kahakura mingled amongst them and joined a group who were threading huge quantities of fish. Surreptitiously, he untied the knots at the end of the lines and soon as fish continued to be threaded, other fish were falling off the lines into the sand.

The fairy folk did not understand what was happening. They busied themselves in rescuing the fish from the sand and were in so much confusion that they failed to notice the setting of the moon and the first glimmers of sunshine from the rising sun. Suddenly, one let out a cry. The sun was up! They must away! In the scurry to depart, one of the nets lay forgotten on the sand.

Kahakura found himself alone, in the morning sunshine, alone with the precious net! He picked it up and ran it carefully through his hands. He saw how simple but effective the idea was. He knew his people could easily replicate such a device and it would revolutionize the village life. He made his way back to the village and arrived just as the sun was going down. With the whole village watching, he demonstrated using the net in the sea and hauled up a load of fish. The villagers were overjoyed and celebrated with music and song.

Themes in the story

This is a story I have used many different times, in many different settings. It describes the eternal theme of striving for a better life. It is a technology story about discovering more efficient ways of doing things, but the answer to Kahakura's problem of how to fish more efficiently comes from his unconscious in the form of a dream (see also the story of the healing waters in Chapter 5). He has to trust that the answer to his problem will come even if some members of the village are sceptical. When he finally discovers the solution, he still has to solve the problem of how to obtain the net from the fairy folk. Here again he thinks creatively. Kahakura didn't go and confront the problem head-on. He didn't go and ask the fairy folk outright or rush in and grab the net. He approached the problem from a different angle, laterally, just as the students in the example given below did.

Ideas for the story

Take pieces of coloured card, draw fish on them, cut them out and laminate them. Punch a hole in each fish and give each child a 'line' to fish with. Make sure there is a knot at the end of each line. The laminated fish have many possibilities. I used them originally with a new group whom I wanted to really look around and explore their environment. So I stuck the fish all around the room with blu-tac and they had to go and find as many as they could and string them on their lines. When all the fish have been caught, we come back to the circle and hold up our line to show everyone and count our fish. Obviously, there is a lot of hand–eye coordination needed to thread the fish, but as usual, we can use hand-over-hand assistance for the less able students. Additionally or alternatively, you can stretch a piece of sea-like fabric between students seated in a circle and throw the fish onto the fabric. Instruct the students to hold on to the fabric with one hand and go fishing with the other.

Once all the fish have been caught I explain that we have to share the fish with the rest of the people in the village. Some children find this difficult. This moment in the enactment of the story was particularly tense for a group of refugee children with whom I worked. Afterwards I could see that the culture of the village described in the story was very different to the culture of the refugee camp where all these children had been raised in a struggle for survival. If a student is resistant to sharing, do not worry and do not insist. The drama sessions return to this theme again and again and the student quickly learns that there is plenty of praise for sharing. The fish are put on the fire (see below), cooked and quickly eaten. I then ask if anyone is still hungry. This is the cue for a brief discussion about how few fish we can catch with just a line and there must be a better way to catch fish.

Sometimes we make a fire on which to cook the laminated fish. A fire occurs in a number of the stories and is fun to make. It consists of a couple of bigger pieces of wood – driftwood is good – and some twigs. One of the pieces of wood has a very convenient cleft where I thread a piece of gold gauze similar to the kind used in the wrapping of flowers or gift wrapping. The flames are red feathers. The major distinguishing feature of a fire, i.e. heat, is absent so students have to be constantly reminded not to lie too close or step in the 'fire', but it works dramatically as a prop and it provides the students with the opportunity to set a fire, something which many of them don't get to do in real life.

The journey across land was one of the features that originally attracted me to the story. It can take whatever form you fancy. I usually have the students follow me through the classroom modelling for them what to do, for example, hacking through forest or wading through streams. I like to explore different levels, but always check with the class teacher about walking on seats or over and under tables, as this might directly countermand what she has been trying to teach students about classroom etiquette.

The original myth had Kahakura as a lone individual making the journey, outwitting the fairies and returning in triumph. I usually name him as the key figure who has the dream, but have him ask for volunteers to go with him. Normally, everyone wants to go, but anyone who wants to can stay at home. The students need to see that any choices are real choices and act accordingly.

This is a great story for practising tying and untying knots and distinguishing night from day. In order for many students to understand the significance of night and day, you will need to make it dramatic. Have someone play the moon (I usually use a mask and starry fabric), who begins by standing on a chair and gradually lowers herself onto the floor where she changes into a sun mask and gold fabric, gets back on the chair and stretches up as tall as she can.

Sometimes a teacher will take a central question in a story and have a discussion with her class in between sessions which I can integrate into the next session. One such discussion was initiated by a teacher of a class of 8-year-olds with Asperger syndrome. It focused on ways of getting the fishing net. In the session, they had tried asking nicely. I paused at this strategy because I obviously wanted to reinforce good manners, but at the same time, I wanted them to understand that just because you ask nicely, this does not guarantee you will get what you want. So I asked the fairy to take her net and chase after the student, catch him and take him back to fairyland.

They also tried snatching the net and running away and again the fairy caught the offending child and took him back to fairyland. In the meantime, the class discussed strategies and came up with a truly original idea. The idea was to throw a cat at the fairy because she would stop to catch the cat and in the meantime, they would escape with the precious net. The essence of the idea is very close to the original story, as it is a distracting/diversionary tactic. They had all drawn pictures of the cat, coloured them in and cut them out so that they were ready to try out this idea. I knew that they were a very competitive group, constantly fighting for adult attention, so I had an idea of where I wanted the story to go.

I gave the staff member playing the fairy my idea and off we went. I asked who wanted to throw their cat and Tony volunteered first. He approached the fairy, shouted, 'Catch!' threw the cat and grabbed the net. The 'fairy' grabbed the cat, carefully put it down and then pursued Tony, eventually catching him and retrieving the net. I said, 'I think the cat idea is the way to go but it doesn't work with just one cat as she has time to catch up and grab the net. What should we do? How can we keep her occupied for longer?' It did not take long for Bernard to come up with the idea that they should all throw their cats and then they worked out how to orchestrate it so that they threw their cats one after the other while Maurice managed to get away with the net. There was a genuine sense of achievement at the end and I felt one of my goals had been met which was to encourage them to work as a team to reach a common goal. We want to encourage lateral, creative thinking and that is what the teacher did. She did not discount the suggestion to use cats as a diversionary tactic and in doing so, affirmed her students and gave them the opportunity to try out the idea for themselves to see whether it worked.

Chapter 11

Devising stories
A Guide to Using Stories
to Explore Themes in Everyday Life

There are some groups where it may be more appropriate to devise stories rather than use traditional stories. These groups are students with an intellectual disability who are developmentally adolescent, adolescents with behavioural issues, and students with nonverbal learning disabilities like Asperger syndrome.

Adolescent students with an intellectual disability

A difficulty for adolescents with a learning disability is that they do not understand the cues essential for the complex ways of interacting with peers. This can result in inappropriate comments or responses. Csoti (2000) suggests the use of social stories because desired reactions can be embedded in the story. Chesner (1995) and Jennings (1995) also support the use of stories to develop social skills in adolescents. Devising stories from material provided by the group helps students make direct connections between the scenes explored in class and their real-life experience. In a session where we were exploring the theme 'two people and a conflict' Lei told us about an incident at the park where a man tried to get her to go with him in his car. It was clear as Lei described the incident that she enjoyed talking about it and she seemed quite gleeful and excited. She reiterated several times how she said 'No' very firmly and pulled her arm away from the stranger. She did not appear traumatized by what had happened. I was thrilled because it was very unusual for Lei to make links between what we were doing in drama and the rest of her life. The ability to generalize, as we have said, is often impaired in students with a learning disability.

In order to get the most out of the sessions there are a number of things to bear in mind. One is that for many young people with a learning disability the ability to act with spontaneity and to think creatively may be impaired.

Johnson (1981) defines spontaneity as:

the ability to act responsively to situations: it necessitates a degree of self confidence, emotional control, and adaptive capability. Therefore, the individual's level of spontaneity in role playing can be used as a general measure of the individual's mental functioning. (p.16)

This means that warm-ups need to stimulate the brain as well as the body. Here are a number of warm-ups that work well with this client group and can be easily adapted to suit the needs of many different individuals.

1. *Name two things* One person sits in the middle of the circle with their eyes closed. A ball is passed around the circle and when the person in the middle shouts, 'Stop,' the person with the ball must name two foods, two places, or two colours in 20 seconds. If he can't he has to go in the middle.

2. *Cornflakes* The group sits in a circle and one person is in the middle. That person calls out, 'Everyone with shoes on, move!' and everyone to whom that applies has to change seats while the person in the middle has to grab a seat. If anyone calls 'Cornflakes,' everyone has to move.

3. *Give a balloon to pairs of students* They have to keep the balloon in the air without touching it by bouncing it between their heads. Then organize a race between pairs holding the balloon between their foreheads as they cross the room. They must hold their hands behind their backs to avoid using them. In the same pairs, give them balls that they have to hold between their backs as they cross the room, holding their hands in front of them.

4. *Bow wow* Ask students to sit in a circle with one student in the middle, blindfolded. In front of the student (the dog) there is a stick (the bone). When the teacher points at a student, he must creep up on the 'dog' as quietly as he can and try to grab the 'bone'. The 'dog' cannot see but listens for any sign and can point in any direction and say, 'Bow wow.' If he points directly at an approaching student, that student out and someone else has a turn.

5. *Making a shape* Divide the group into threes and call out a shape for them to make as a group. Examples are a letter of the alphabet, numbers, a table and chair, a flower, a dragon, the Eiffel tower.

I teach a variety of drama structures that convey emotion and information about the scene but do not rely on verbal skills, which are likely to be a weak point for many students. Drama conventions such as sculpting, simple mimes and freeze-framing are invaluable because they do not require dialogue.

SCULPTING

Divide into pairs with one person as the 'sculptor' and the other the 'clay'. The job of the clay is to be an amazing substance that is flexible while retaining the shape into which it is put by the sculptor. The job of the sculptor is to gently mould the clay into the shape of a specific word. The sculptor does this by physically moving the clay's limbs and adjusting its posture. He can discreetly show the clay what facial expression he wants by doing it himself and have the clay mirror it. The clay has to hold the shape while we try to guess the word, and can then relax. Sometimes I will ask the clay what it felt like to be moulded or to assume that shape. These questions are designed to increase the students' awareness of taking and abdicating control and how our thoughts and feelings are affected by how we hold ourselves physically.

MIMING

Simple mimes of everyday activities familiar to students are a good way to begin devising stories. To support this we begin with a brainstorm around the whiteboard where we think of examples of everyday activities. Then each student chooses one to mime to the others, for which he gets a point and whoever guesses the mime gets a point. Extra support is given where appropriate and I sometimes give a little input on basic mime skills, for example shaping the hand according to what you are carrying or demonstrating by your body language if something is heavy or light.

You can develop this further by getting students to work in pairs to mime a simple activity. When they perform for the group ask them to freeze the action and then ask the group for suggestions of what each person might be saying. Choose a short line for each person, get him to repeat it until he can remember it and then unfreeze the action and get him to say his lines while performing the action. Follow with uproarious applause. In this way, you have created a simple scene with dialogue and you can continue to build scenes in this way until you have created a story.

The secret is to keep scenes short. This applies both to scenes which are created in the moment and to those which you give students time to plan.

This is because although students may be capable of planning longer, more complex scenes, there are some who will have a tendency to forget what was planned in the process of an enactment. This can be frustrating and undermining to their confidence.

FREEZE FRAMES

When a group has developed some confidence and skills, I ask them to devise scenes around a specific theme, for example, an emotion like anger. We will first discuss situations where someone may get angry, to give students ideas. They then need to plan a scene and rehearse freezing it at a specific point where the theme is most clearly expressed. Sometimes students are so absorbed in acting out the scene that I need to call out 'Freeze.' Freezing the action is a good way to stop the scene at the point of the greatest learning and avoid rambling, which can occur when a student has forgotten what he was supposed to do, but feels too awkward to say.

Although dialogue is limited with these students, I work with them on making it count. I encourage students to deliver their dialogue, even if it is just one word, clearly and with conviction. Although the emphasis is not on improving their verbal communication, paradoxically, it clearly improves as their confidence grows.

Adolescent students with attentional or behavioural problems

Although we have left the 'long ago and far away' land of the traditional story, we continue to utilize the distancing techniques that are a common characteristic of drama therapy. We can see clearly here how drama therapy used in this way differs from psychodrama, in that students do not play themselves and stories are not focused on real incidents in their lives.

When beginning to devise a story I usually ask the group to suggest a location, and out of those suggestions, I choose the one I think has the most dramatic potential and opportunities for learning. For example, I had several students who regularly absconded and spent time with street kids. The issues then became ones of survival, so I would usually choose a location that involved potential danger. I then asked for a character, a young girl or boy who is no older than the oldest student in the room. We give them a name, avoiding actual names of people in the group, as we still want to maintain some distance. We are aiming to keep the story within the experience of the students but not so close that it is unbearably confronting.

With adolescents, disabled or otherwise, a story needs to be obviously relevant to those in the group. A distinguishing feature of adolescence is self-consciousness. Young people want to look 'cool' and are extremely sensitive to the opinions of peers. What this means is that they will not get up in front of a group and risk possible humiliation unless they can see the relevance of what we are doing. Stanislavski (1949) espoused the importance of the student experiencing the similarity between the self and the role. Wilkinson said that 'the perceived role must provide opportunities for meaningful action which relate to the student's capabilities and experience. Out of this arises commitment to the experience and a sense of control within one's limits. (1980, p.47)' This is why we have abandoned the oblique method of the traditional story in favour of the use of dramatic distance in a contemporary story.

However, the very proximity of the self and the role, particularly if the student has been used to working within the safety of a traditional story, can produce anxiety that may express itself in a reluctance to participate or disruptive behaviour. 'This fear of entering the unknown quality of the "here and now" presents a risk of failure and humiliation to the individual' (Landy, 1986, pp.105–6). Fear of failure is one of the major reasons why a group or an individual student will refuse to participate and this puts the onus on the facilitator to see where that fear can be alleviated by the teaching of skills and the creation of a culture of encouragement.

As always in drama therapy, we aim for the small incremental steps that gradually increase confidence, working in the gap between the known and the unknown, just outside the comfort zone. This is what Vygotsky called the 'proximal zone' which he described as the 'actual developmental level as determined by independent problem solving and the level of potential development as determined through problem solving under adult guidance or in collaboration with more capable peers' (Vygotsky, 1978, p.103).

Finding the gap the between the known and the unknown may be problematic with adolescents as they may mask insecurity with a show of bravado. If you are meeting resistance and a reluctance to participate, it is probably because you are asking too much too soon and not that you are asking too little. Adapt accordingly and meet them where they are (without making it too obvious). When working with adolescents you need great skills to be able to read the group because often they don't say what they mean. When they say, 'This is boring,' you need to judge whether they mean it. The main thing is to use the suggestions they make and not start censoring them. You may need to speak to support staff about the reasons for this.

Basically, if you want to stimulate input so that the students 'own' the material worked on in the sessions you have to take whatever they offer you and run with it, otherwise you will notice a drop in energy.

In one group, the students were divided into small groups each working with a teacher aide and the theme of the scene was 'what young people do at the weekend'. One student who was usually very reluctant to speak up suggested a scene that involved taking drugs and the teacher aide said, 'No, we're not doing that.' The student got up and left the classroom a short time later. Unless it is a specific injunction of the place where you are working, for example a drug and substance abuse programme where students are forbidden to talk about their drug use outside specific parameters, I would not censor a scene involving drugs. We are not condoning or trivializing its use in allowing students to play out what they know and give us an opportunity to explore the consequences and in some cases the antecedents.

Drama is ideal for the ADHD child who needs lots of stimulation and to be physically engaged. The student who is always acting out can see a way to finally legitimately have an audience. You have to ensure that he can see that he has to obey certain rules and work within certain parameters in order to get the attention he craves. It is an excellent way for impulsive or anti-social students to explore the consequences of actions on themselves and others. Drama is an infinitely flexible medium. It allows us to explore the future, or a range of possible futures, if we wish. This is useful for adolescents who live very much in the moment and who have problems imagining a future.

I worked with a group of boys with conduct disorder. On one occasion, we were having an individual session with me, another member of staff and Clive, one of the group. I asked him about his aspirations and his hopes for the future. Any concept of future was noticeably lacking when asked about in the group setting. I had assumed that was partly due to the disorder and partly a natural corollary of being an adolescent, but it made exploring consequences difficult as students in the group could rarely imagine them. However, on this occasion, when I asked Clive what he wanted to be, he responded immediately 'an ice hockey player'. He had only just started lessons but it clearly grabbed his imagination. The three of us started to devise a story of 'Mike', an ice hockey player. In the role of 'Mike' Clive scored numerous goals for his team. We acted out the scene with the staff member playing the 'opposing team' and me as commentator. Clive wanted to enact the part where he scored the winning goals again and again. I was happy to do that as hitherto Clive's means of getting attention had been destructive and anti-social. It reminded me of the beginnings of the collaborative play of much younger children. Clive's mother had had schizophrenia and his attachment to her had been fraught with difficulty. He had never had a secure base from which to venture into play with other children.

I said to him that every story needs to have some difficulty or challenge in it to make it interesting. I was wondering what 'Mike's' challenges were. Clive thought for a moment and then said, 'He gets cancer.' I asked him how Mike discovers he has cancer and he said they found it out when he had an accident on the ice. We enacted the accident and the later interview with the doctor when 'Mike' was told the news of his cancer.

We all played our parts with absolute integrity. There was none of the silliness and abusive language Clive was accustomed to using. Our session was ending and I didn't want to leave the story in the hospital with Mike battling cancer. I told Clive, Mike recovers and goes on to play international ice hockey. How long does Clive think it takes Mike to recover his form? 'Five years,' said Clive. 'It took him three years to recover fully from the cancer and another two years to build his fitness back and start competing again.'

I am quite taken aback by such an appropriate response. This student has real problems delaying gratification and controlling his impulses. Yet he has learnt that in the pursuit of a goal, we need persistence and hard work and it often takes time to get where we want to go. The drama enabled him to see and feel what it is like to achieve a goal. Imagining is the first step towards creating a future. Enacting different possibilities increased his resourcefulness and helped to focus all that restless energy.

The story is not really about how to become an ice hockey player. It is about how to have an image of the future. When young people feel they have no future, they become dangerous and destructive because they feel they have nothing to lose. Drama therapy gives them the opportunity to play with images of a whole variety of different futures as well as exploring problems and possibilities in the here and now.

Here are examples of some warm-ups I have used with adolescent groups. I have found that the quicker we start moving around the more engaged the students become. Do not give them time to think of a reason why they should not participate. Games that have a competitive edge seem to work best.

1. *Red light/green light* or *Stop 'n' go.* One player stands at the front of the class with his back turned and car keys on the floor just behind

his feet. The students line up behind him and their goal is to creep up and get the keys without getting 'out'. A student is out if he is caught moving when the first player turns around. Prior to turning, the player calls out either 'stop' or 'red light' and when he turns back to face the wall, the cue for the students to commence creeping is 'green light' or 'go'. If a student is 'out' and sent back, he can start again. One class so loved this game that we played it every week for a term. Each week I tried to make it harder by adding obstacles the students had to navigate around before they could snatch the keys. These included chairs students had to sit on, a pole they had to balance on and a table they had to crawl under.

There are many variations on this game. These include teaming up with two others, linking arms, with the person in the middle closing his eyes. Then they must advance as a team, so if one of them moves during a 'red' light they will all be sent back to start again. There is a group version where students play as individuals up until the point that someone successfully manages to snatch the keys and then they must work as a team to pass the keys back to the starting point without the first player spotting which person has possession of them. If the first player successfully identifies which of the team has the keys, all students must return to the start, but if he guesses incorrectly, the game continues.

2. A *tug-of-war* is always good, particularly with boys. You can use this simple exercise to encourage them to analyse why a team won. Did they crouch down low? Put their strongest player at the back? Was there a point where they all decided that they *could* win?

3. The rope you use in the tug of war can then be used to play *Cliff top*, which is a game where everyone stands on the rope as it lies flat on the floor and imagines that they are on the edge of a cliff with a sheer drop at either side. The object is then to organize themselves into order of height or age or whatever without stepping off the rope.

4. *Ball games* are always good. Bring in two or three or more balls and start a simple pass around where you have to say the other person's name as you throw it to him. Then add a second ball where you have to name a food, which can then not be mentioned twice. Add extra balls where you have to name a part of the world or a tv programme which again cannot be mentioned more than once.

5. *Pegs.* Each person has a peg pinned to his back and students have to grab as many as they can without getting their peg grabbed.

6. *Ping pong.* Give everyone a paper plate and stand in a circle. Bounce the ping pong ball around the circle without dropping it, using the plate. Divide into teams and the object is for each member of the team to hit the ball at least once and then sit down. First team to finish, wins.

7. *Sharks and islands.* Place newspaper on the floor and play music. Students must move around the space and when the music stops, find an island (piece of newspaper) and stand on it. Anyone who can't find space on an island is eaten by sharks. Reduce the amount of newspaper as the game progresses. I usually encourage players to try to save each other and give points for those who do.

Boundaries are extremely important with this client group. Discuss with the group a set of guidelines and then be vigilant to enforce them. In work with extremely disturbed adolescents, you may need to use more structure. There are some excellent ideas in James Thompson's (1999) book *Drama Workshops for Anger Management and Offending Behaviour.*

Students with Asperger syndrome

The DSM IV diagnostic criteria for Asperger syndrome disorder lists impairments in social interaction such as lack of social or emotional reciprocity and impairments in nonverbal behaviours such as body posture, facial expression and gestures to regulate social interaction. This is one reason why activities like drama, which focus on both verbal and nonverbal communication and on role-play, are so useful for the student with Asperger syndrome. Although one class I had participated very enthusiastically in sessions where I used traditional stories, I felt that this more indirect way of exploring human relationships was not as appropriate as addressing social skills in a very direct way. I began with a discussion about feelings. This included emotions like anger, sadness and happiness, and physical feelings like hunger, tiredness and feeling sick. I then demonstrated with a staff member, 'sculpting' her into a specific feeling we had already discussed. I chose an easy one like 'happy' and deliberately made her facial expression and posture very exaggerated so that it would be easier to see. One student picked the right answer straightaway, while others offered words like 'sick' or 'angry'. The students were very keen to have a turn themselves and although I had planned to have them working in pairs together, I discovered the group worked best if we all watched a pair working in the centre of the circle and then had a go at guessing what the word was. We made it into a game where whoever guessed what someone was trying to sculpt had the next go and could choose the person he wanted to be his 'clay'. The students enjoyed this activity so much that we continued for several sessions. I laminated words like falling, relaxed, and eating and they had to choose one to sculpt. Students really enjoyed being shown the word when they had correctly guessed it.

Sculpting works really well with this client group as it enables the student to see the effects of where he is placing the other student and it encourages students to work together which was something they rarely wanted to do.

To develop this idea we brainstormed situations where we might be sad or angry and put a selection of them up on the whiteboard. One person chose a situation and sculpted a number of people to convey this situation. One student in particular loved having the opportunity to be in charge of a number of his classmates. We developed this into short role-plays, at each stage stopping to check that someone was conveying what he intended to convey. We gave students hand mirrors to check their facial expressions. Working in small groups, the students had to choose a situation and play out the scene so that it was very clear to an audience what the dominant emotion was.

Warm-ups with this group can be tricky as you may have students who react very badly to losing in games involving competitiveness. I have found the following to work really well.

1. *Change three things.* Get students to work in pairs. One closes his eyes while the other changes three things about his appearance. When the student opens his eyes, he has to identify what the three things were. This is a good game to challenge students to look at each other.

2. *Horse race.* Everyone stands in a circle and follows instructions. A trot is indicated by slapping one's thighs which can be sped up to a gallop, leaning to the right and leaning to the left; over the jump everyone lifts arms in the air and shouts 'Whoa', through the river, everyone pats hand on mouth to make a whooping sound. Students can take it in turns to shout instructions.

3. *Wind, tree, crow.* Everyone stands in a circle with one person in the middle. He points to someone in the circle and together with the

person on either side they have to make the shape of either the wind (students link arms, sway and make wind sound), the tree (the two students on either side stand behind a third person and lift his arms up to make the branches of a tree) or the crow (the middle person extends his arms out straight like a beak while the other two make a wing on either side). The leader counts to see how fast students can react with the correct shape.

As always it is important to have fun and to affirm the behaviour you want in whatever way feels comfortable to you. I find a tick chart works well, even with the older students, affirming behaviour like listening, playing by the rules and teamwork and verbally affirming examples of these throughout the session.

12

Using a Visual Storyboard
with Students with Autism

Those whose perceptions remain concrete and firmly based in the here and now can be confused by full blown imaginary work. They might still be able to find their place within a group enactment by relating at a sensory level rather than a narrative level to the activity. (Chesner, 1995, p.137)

For many students with autism, the physical, active elements of the session provide fun and the repetitious elements provide security. Many autistic students will participate after several sessions when they begin to recognize the facilitator and can trust that they do not have to do anything they do not want to do. The drama session may be one of the few group activities that the autistic student participates in and it provides an invaluable opportunity for the student to interact with others.

It may, however, resemble a series of activities of which the student cannot make sense without an understanding of the narrative, which is, after all, the thread that links the whole session together. An understanding of narrative teaches students two important things.

First, there is a causal link between events, which means that some things are predictable and can be anticipated. This is extremely important information for the autistic student to have. An understanding of narrative helps an autistic student to realize that his actions can influence events both positively and negatively. Here the student moves from what is essentially a fatalistic, deterministic position in the world to one where he sees he can have an effect. This is extremely empowering. Where previously the student felt he could only react to events which often made no sense to him, he now has more options available to him.

Second, an understanding of narrative teaches that there is a reason for a person's emotional response to an event; people do not usually react chaotically and unpredictably. The student can then begin to make sense of the human interactions that are often simplified in stories and this further aids comprehension. The extreme anxiety often displayed and described by students with autism can be a result of not knowing what is going to happen next in a world where they are unable to interpret information received from their senses. For autistic students, and those who are very literal and have problems understanding abstractions, a storyboard is a good way of assisting comprehension of the narrative of the story. The use of a storyboard can deepen and enhance their experience and help to make sense of the activities in the session that may have seemed random or inexplicable before when there had been no understanding of the narrative. The storyboard makes the story into a kind of visual journey that the student can explore with his teacher and then examine in his own time as often as he wants.

The storyboard

The storyboard is designed to be introduced to students prior to the session by the class teacher. It is a mixture of very simple narrative accompanied by visuals. It can also be used as a story in its own right and the teacher can experiment with how many times they need to go through the story prior to the session, depending on the response of the students.

The first step is to choose a story that has images to which the students can relate, and a very simple structure. I am using the example of 'The bell of Hamana' which can be found on page 46 in a fuller version.

What follows is a précis of the story that was written in collaboration with a class teacher who was very knowledgeable about what aspects of the story her students would understand and could be included. For example, in the fuller version, we are told that the tortoise will die because he is stuck upside down. She told me that her students would not understand the word 'die' and indeed dying is a very abstract concept for many children, not just those with autism. We decided to use something within the experience of the students that would help them to comprehend the seriousness of the situation. These students had no problem understanding that not being able to eat or drink would make the tortoise very sad. Again, the description of the tortoise as wise is omitted and the fact that the tortoise is repaying an earlier kindness is simplified to the brief phrase 'he is my friend'.

The story was typed out in a 36-point font with two phrases appearing on each A4 piece of paper. Each page also included visuals. These were laminated photographs or symbols familiar to students, which were attached to the page with Velcro strips so that they could be removed with ease and passed around the group for them to look at. Some ingenuity was needed to get the photograph of the man pushing the tortoise over. This required a trip to the zoo to get a photograph of a Galapagos tortoise and a photo session with a friend posing in my garden as the woodcutter. In one photo, he squatted down with his hands in the right position to be pushing a large object and we cut and pasted this with the photo of the tortoise. Digital cameras make this process incredibly easy and the Internet provides access to many images that can be legitimately downloaded and used.

The bell of Hamana

This is a story about a forest.

This man chops wood in the forest.

The man goes into the forest. This is a tortoise.

The man sees the tortoise but the tortoise is upside down.

The tortoise is very sad.
The tortoise cannot eat or drink.
The tortoise says to the man, 'Please help me.'
The man pushes the tortoise.

The man pushes the tortoise over.
The tortoise is very happy.
The tortoise goes back into the forest.
The man starts to chop a tree.

Suddenly there is a big roar.
The man is very scared.

A bear, a tiger and a wolf come.
They are very angry with the man.
They want to hurt him.
They do not like him chopping down all the trees.
Suddenly a voice says, 'Stop!'
The tortoise arrives.
He says, 'Do not hurt this man. He is my friend.'
The tiger, the bear and the wolf leave.
They do not hurt the man.
The man is very happy.
The tortoise says, 'I have a present for you.'
He gives the man a bell.
The man is very happy.

The tortoise says, 'Take this back to your friends and play it so that you can think of me and the tiger, the wolf and the bear.'
The tortoise says, 'Don't chop down too many trees.'

The first session that I trialled using visuals in this way was a marked success. The class teacher had gone through the storyboard with the students the day before and she said they had enjoyed looking at the photographs and were very attentive. When I did the session, I noticed that the appearance of the storyboard, which was a large black book with plastic pocket pages, elicited interest in the group. I found that passing the visuals around helped to focus those group members who were usually restless and it seemed to be stimulating verbal responses from some students. Probably the most useful aspect of the storyboard for me was being able to clarify parts of the story that I know must have appeared incomprehensible to some of the students in previous sessions. For example, usually I would dress a staff member up in the green tube and take a plastic axe and mime chopping him till he fell down. I was now able to hold up the photograph of the tree and to say to students at this point, 'This is Kurt pretending to be a tree. Kurt is pretending to be a tree.' I am almost sure that I saw a dawning realization pass across one particular student's face when he realized what Kurt was doing. I continued, 'I am pretending to be the woodcutter.' The photograph of a woodcutter is circulating at this point. I repeat, 'I am pretending to be a woodcutter and I am pretending to chop down this tree. Kurt is pretending to be the tree.' There were several students who had no concept of pretending and this was clear from what the teacher had observed of their play. The visuals really helped them to understand that that was what we were doing *at the time.* One student in particular looked a little worried when I began to mime chopping down the tree played by the teacher aide, but the more we reiterated, 'We are pretending,' the more relaxed and happy he looked.

The symbols were also invaluable as so many of the students had trouble reading emotion from a human face but the symbol helped to clarify for them what the different characters were feeling. They were then better able to organize their own faces to approximate the specific emotion simplified in the symbol, which was something that they had found difficult to do in previous sessions when I had simply said, 'So-and-so is feeling sad,' and made a sad face.

Many of the stories in this book share similar elements. Several of them share a similar setting or involve the same animals or dramatic features. This means that although it takes quite a lot of work to make the first storyboard, parts of it can then be used in other stories. A challenge is to find images of fairytale characters, but I found I could quite easily improvise. For example, I acquired a good picture of a giant by shooting a picture of my six foot, burly neighbour from the bottom of some stairs!

13

Drama Therapy and Engaging the Attention of Students with an Intellectual Disability
A Research Study

This chapter contains details of research that was carried out as part of a Master of Arts degree in Creative Arts Therapies. The key research question in the study was, 'Does drama therapy engage the attention of students with an intellectual disability?' Four students were identified as target students in a class of eight in a special school. The methodology describes the design of the drama therapy sessions and the methods used to collect information for analysis. The expected result was that the students' attention was engaged during the course of the sessions. It was hoped that their overall attentiveness was improved through their participation and that this ability to pay attention was generalized to other areas. Thus, a supplementary research question was, 'Does participation in drama therapy sessions improve the overall attentiveness of students with an intellectual disability?'

The key findings were that high levels of attentiveness were present in all four of the target students for the duration of the observation sessions. The findings also indicated that a range of social skills were taught and practised by the students during the sessions. There was some evidence that social skills were also generalized to other areas. Levels of attentiveness were consistent after the session with levels before the intervention despite the stimulating nature of the intervention.

Intellectual disability and the importance of attention

Attention is pivotal to cognitive functioning and generally considered a precursory state to the learning of most tasks and the acquisition of skills – cognitive, social-behavioural and language.

> Paying attention and retention are components of the input process in learning. Most exceptional learners can see and hear, but many do not do so when we want them to. Most are capable of retaining what they learn, but may not do so, because they do not pay attention. (Hewett and Forness, 1977, p.380)

A number of authors confirm the prevalence of distractibility in students with an intellectual disability. Patton, Beirne-Smith and Payne identify distractibility and inattentiveness as two of the characteristics most commonly seen in students with mental retardation (cited in Wood and Lazari, 1997, p.434). Keogh and Margolis (cited in Bortoli and Brown, 2002, p.7) go as far as to suggest that attentional disturbances and ineffective attention separates groups of students with disabilities from those without. Students with disabilities are described as having problems with attention span, self-regulation, activity level, impulse control and distractibility (Douglas, 1980; Keogh and Margolis, 1976; Kopp and Vaughn, 1982; Teeter and Semrud-Clikeman, 1997 cited in Bortoli and Brown, 2002, p.5).

Selective attention is a behavioural trait often associated with autism although some researchers identify this as a characteristic of students with an intellectual disability in general. Here the child may be very absorbed in specific activities while uninterested in others and experience difficulty in executing attention shifts. 'In students with an intellectual disability, the ability to shift focus cannot be managed easily, as it places specific cognitive demands on them' (Kasari et al, 1995).

Wood and Lazari define attention as 'the ability to focus on a stimulus and maintain that focus over time' (1997, p.434). They describe four different categories of attention deficits common in students with an intellectual disability. These are over-attention, under-attention, perseveration and over-sensitivity to information. Over-attention makes transitions difficult, as the child cannot shift easily from one activity to another. Under-attention is commonly known as distractibility. It means that the child cannot differentiate between what is important and what is not. Perseveration involves being stuck on a repetitious activity, word or phrase, and over-sensitivity to information is when information received by the senses blocks out all other stimuli and makes it impossible to concentrate on the task in hand.

Ruff and Rothbart (cited in Bortoli and Brown, 2002, p.9) describe attention as a state that is dynamic in nature and involves ignoring external stimuli and increasing effort and concentration. They describe the different states of attention as alertness, focusing, stimulus selection and being able to alternate attention. They emphasize the importance of an executive function that manages one's attention state and moves from one to the other where appropriate. As previously stated, attention shifts are often problematic in students with an intellectual disability.

Bortoli and Brown (2002, p.10) focus on five states which are pivotal to memory, learning and cognition. These are inattention, and attention that is aware/alert, sustained, focused and divided. Inattention is missing significant information in the learning of a task. Alertness is paying attention while maintaining sensitivity to changes in the environment. Sustained attention is the ability to stay on task over a period of time and filter out irrelevant stimuli. Focused attention is being able to focus on a single task while varying levels of concentration. Divided attention is the ability to focus on more than one task at a time.

It is clear from the literature surveyed that attention is not a static state, but a complex series of interrelated components, some of which require a high level of cognitive functioning.

Attention in drama therapy

A relatively small number of practitioners have written academic articles about the relevance of drama therapy for people with an intellectual disability, so there are very few direct references to attention in peer reviews. Is it because the effectiveness of drama therapy in engaging attention is too obvious to even warrant a mention? Or is it perceived as an educational as opposed to a therapeutic issue? This is interesting when you think that a large number of registered drama therapists who are members of the British Association of Dramatherapists are employed in education.

Peter Slade, an educationalist who greatly influenced the development of early British drama therapists with his work on child development and the importance of play, highlights attention and concentration as positive effects of the use of drama with children. 'Drama has a part to play as an aid to confidence, hope, feelings of security, discovery of sympathy, and to concentration' (Slade, 1959, cited in Weaver, 1996/7, p.15). Slade also identifies what he calls 'absorption'. This is a state that he perceives as normal to young children absorbed in play and learning through play, and that he sees as influencing one's ability to 'concentrate, remember and learn' (cited in Weaver, 1996/7, p.15). This state of absorption is one that I aim to create in the students who take part in drama therapy sessions and one I will discuss in more detail later.

Alignment with special education literature

In contrast to the drama therapy literature, the literature of special education abounds with references to attention and implications for learning methods. Referring to the needs of students who are highly distractible, Strauss and Werner (1941) emphasize the importance of a structured programme with a minimum of extraneous stimulation (cited in Hallahan and Kauffman, 1978). Cruikshank (1961) developed these ideas further in a project designed around three principles of structure, reduction of outside stimulation and intensity of teaching materials (cited in Hallahan and Kauffman). His definition of structure is one that is totally teacher directed with the assumption that hyperactive students are incapable of making their own decisions about what activities they want to pursue (ibid.). In the same way, drama therapy takes place within a structure that includes repetitious elements, such as songs that open and close the session. However, it also provides many opportunities for choice, initiation and spontaneity.

In another area of study, Fernald (1943) pioneered the use of multi-sensory approaches and devised the VAKT method (visual, auditory, kinaes-thetic and tactile) which is mostly used in the teaching of reading, spelling and mathematics. 'Multi sensory methods involve the remediation of a child's problems by using a combination of the child's sensory systems in the training process' (cited in Hallahan and Kauffman, 1978, p.150). Likewise, drama therapy uses props that the students can see, feel and play with. For example, varieties of masks are used that have visual and tactile appeal. The students can look at someone else wearing them, try them on and look at themselves, experiment with noises that accompany them or simply explore the mask with their hands.

Echoing Cruikshank, Hewett and Forness stress the importance of intensifying teaching material. 'In teaching children who have problems paying attention or retaining what they learn, we are concerned with increasing the vividness or impact of the task and with emphasising its concrete aspects' (1977, p.380). Drama therapy uses stories which are chosen because they lend themselves to a physical interpretation of themes. Students go on journeys, they wriggle through tunnels and climb over rocks.

In addition, educationalists emphasize that 'the more salient the stimulus, and the more interesting and compelling the stimulus, the greater is its functional value in gaining the attention of the observer' (Cole and Chan, 1990, p.198). Correspondingly, drama therapy uses props chosen for their potential to appeal to the students, but the other major feature of the session that engages the attention is the drama therapist herself. She uses variations in her voice, facial expression and physical presence to engage and retain the attention of the students.

Current thinking in education is that interactive teaching methods are also an effective component with this population. Interactive methods can include 'semi-ritualized structures' or 'meta-scripts' (Westera, 2002, p.51), which make them effective with young children, people for whom English is a second language and students with an intellectual disability. These features include structure that is 'not so prescriptive that there is no room for responsive teaching' (Palincsar, 1995, cited in Westera, 2002, p.51) and this also applies to observational learning and student participation. Interactive methods provide a structure within which choice and initiative can be offered to the student in small achievable tasks. This is also the preferable way to engage the unresponsive student who is also likely to be in the class. Within a 35-minute drama therapy session, the student is involved in a number of different but associated activities within a familiar structure.

In an attempt to review effective practices within special education, King-Sears (1997, cited in Westera, 2002, p.26) identifies ten practices 'which have the greatest desired impact in affective, psychomotor and cognitive areas of academics for students with and without disabilities'. Of these, eight could be considered aligned to drama therapy techniques as used in the current study. These are cooperative learning, differentiated instruction, self- determination, explicit instruction, collaboration, proactive behaviour management, peer supports and generalization techniques.

Wood and Lazari identify six adaptations that need to be made in order to engage the student with learning disabilities. These include classroom structure, time management, grouping structures, student engagement, direct instruction and interactive teaching (1997, p.145). These six adaptations all feature in the delivery of a drama therapy session, as well as other features of best teaching practice such as direct teaching of content, modelling of skills, guided practice followed by independent practice, feedback and active learner involvement.

Summary of literature review

The review of the literature clearly revealed a lack of research by drama therapy practitioners with students with an intellectual disability. What research was available did not explore the effectiveness of drama therapy methods in retaining the attention of students with an intellectual disability. A link between intellectual disability and distractibility was shown, including the importance of attention in the process of learning. The features of the drama therapy session that retain the attention were outlined and aligned with the work of educational researchers on best teaching methods for this population.

Components of the drama therapy sessions

Specific components of the drama therapy session were considered to enhance the likelihood of engaging the attention of the students. There were four such components.

The first component is the student's familiarity with the structure of the session. The basic structure of a drama therapy session is warm-up, main event and closure. The warm-up is the part of the session where the students are greeted and prepared for their participation in the main event. The main event is the enactment of a part of the story using props and tasks rehearsed in the warm-up. The closure signals the end of the session and usually involves taking off roles (known as de-roling) and reaffirming one's own identity in preparation for moving on to other activities in the timetable. In addition, each session began with a very brief reminder of the presence of the observer.

The second component is the use of traditional stories. Each session was designed around a specific, traditional story that took place over three sessions. Over the six sessions, two stories were used, 'Rata' and 'Paikea' (Orbell, 1992, pp.40–88). Using a traditional story optimizes attention span for a number of reasons. It provides a structure that the students can recognize. It has a beginning, middle and end, a central character or group and easily recognizable archetypal characters such as the hero, the monster and the trickster. Traditional stories often contain simple themes like good versus evil and the importance of helping and not harming others. These themes are easily understood by the students and reinforce the teaching of values and social skills. The central character or group has a task to perform in the face of sometimes seemingly insurmountable obstacles. A conflict of some sort drives the dramatic tension since 'conflict resides at the heart of virtually every folktale' (Durrell and Sachs, 1990, cited in Gersie, 1997, p.24). In a fun and interactive way, the story teaches students about the importance of cooperation, persistence and the satisfaction of achieving shared goals. Group social skills are taught and practised in every session. 'The way a position is taken, how it is defended and how a character relates to the other party's point of view enhances or defuses the conflict situation' (Goforth and Spillmann, 1994, cited in Gersie, 1997, p.24).

Another way in which a traditional story captures attention is in its relevance to the student. 'The story's apparently incidental relevance enables the teller to elicit and sustain the listener's agreement to attend to the tale' (Gersie, 1997, p.8). Common themes used with this population are stories that feature unlikely heroes, small, underestimated creatures or characters undervalued by their community. These characters triumph in the course of the story and are recognized for their true value by the people around them. These stories are attractive to students who may have feelings of powerlessness and inferiority associated with their disability.

Many of the traditional stories used were culturally relevant to some of the students in the class. Traditional stories give information about the culture from which they come, the customs, the beliefs, the language and the dilemmas. Using traditional stories from a variety of cultures encouraged respect for differences and explored issues of diversity in an engaging way that students could understand.

Stories contain themes that are developmentally relevant for the student, and as previously stated, may mirror some of the issues in the student's life. This can be as simple as being a small person in a big person's world. In contrast, stories that are too sophisticated, subtle or that involve too much dialogue, were considered unsuitable and avoided.

The traditional stories used provided opportunities for interactive, dramatic play. These opportunities are presented as achievable 'tasks' that are modelled by the therapist using limited and simplified verbal instruction accompanied by encouragement and followed by applause. As a predictable feature of the session, students quickly learned that they needed to pay attention to the modelling done by the therapist or they would be unable to perform the task accurately in front of an audience (the other members of the group). The stories had kinaesthetic possibilities such as getting up and doing something like going on a journey or building a spider's web or creeping up on a monster. They involved the use of props, masks and basic costumes. These appeal to the students because they are brightly coloured, intriguing and they can handle them, wear them, and experience them with their senses.

The third component is the level of involvement of the therapist and the support staff. The students observe the staff's level of involvement and react accordingly. They must maintain the integrity and conviction of the imaginative world they create and when this happens, the students are more likely to become absorbed in the drama and give it their full attention as they are influenced by the attention behaviour of the people around them. A playful, encouraging atmosphere where firm boundaries are maintained is essential to engage the attention of the students. The therapist uses voice, face and body to clarify for the students what the emotional tone of the story is and thus aids comprehension and engagement. 'In the final analysis, the effectiveness of models and modalities, of approaches and tools, hinges on the personal characteristics of the practitioner who applies them' (Emunah, 1994, p. xxi).

The fourth component is the environmental factors that affect the quality of the student's attention. They include delineating space, seating arrangements and removing distractions. The students are seated upright in chairs in a semi-circle facing the therapist. They are strategically placed next to a support person or a student with whom they are compatible. The therapist requests that there be no interruptions from outside the classroom. These environmental factors combine to create what the renowned theatre director, writer and politician Augusto Boal refers to as 'aesthetic space', which is whatever has been designated as restricted space within which action takes place. 'The aesthetic space possesses...properties, which stimulate knowledge and discovery, cognition and recognition: properties which stimulate the process of *learning by experience*' (Boal, 1995, p.20). He goes on to say that,

> the aesthetic space thus comes into being because the combined attention of a whole audience converges upon it...This force of attraction is aided by the very structure of theatres...which oblige the spectators all to look in the same direction; and it is abetted by the simple presence of actors and spectators who connive in their acceptance of the theatrical codes and their participation in the celebration of the show. (Boal, 1995, p.19)

Participants and setting

Four students, their classmates, teacher and two teacher aides participated in this study. The four target students were aged 6 and 7 years old. Four other students in the class also took part in the drama sessions as per their regular timetable. Excluded from the study were any students receiving medication to improve attention, e.g. Ritalin. All students had Individual Education Plans and a moderate to severe intellectual disability.

Anne is 6 years old and of New Zealand European ethnicity. She is developmentally delayed. She is long sighted, wears glasses, has mild to moderate hearing loss in both ears and wears a hearing aid. She has difficulties with her balance and spatial awareness. She can be resistant to direction but this means she is also sometimes more determined to complete a task than others in the class. In addition, she is keen to please so can usually be distracted if the focus is redirected onto another child in the class. She loves school but is usually tired by the end of the week when her behaviour can deteriorate. She can construct sentences but prefers to use single words and communicate nonverbally. For example, she will get the sign for an activity she wants to do and when the teacher models the appropriate phrase, 'I want to play on the computer', Anne concurs rather than repeats the sentence for herself. Her attention is distracted by the behaviour of other students.

Tom is 6 years old and of New Zealand European ethnicity. He has Autistic Spectrum Disorder characteristics and dislikes change. For instance, he usually resists transitions from one activity to another. He is affectionate but can be aggressive if compliance is insisted on although this is usually only when his anxiety is high. He enjoys activities with lots of movement and can be rough. He can rote count to 100, compose simple sentences and responds to the Picture Exchange Communication System very well. He is distracted by changes in routine or his environment.

David is 7 years old and of New Zealand European ethnicity. He has Down syndrome. He is a passive little boy who tends not to initiate. He has a heart murmur, low muscle tone and weakness in his neck, which means caution must be exercised with vigorous and forceful activities. He is very quiet but can be non-compliant. He lacks confidence in his speaking, his speech is unclear and he whispers single words. He has a short attention span and needs prompting to pay attention.

Steven is 7 years old and of Maori ethnicity. He has Down syndrome. He can be rough with other children and may throw things but his behaviour has much improved while he has been in school. In whole-class teacher-directed situations Steven will participate by watching and following the other children. He mimics and listens to isolated words to follow directions. He interacts at a very early level of communication and has some hearing impairment. He has a short attention span and is easily distracted by visitors to the classroom.

Research design

The research design is a descriptive case study supplemented with a range of qualitative and quantitative data. Measures were used before, during and after the drama therapy sessions. The quantitative measures used were a pre- and post-test and observation record. The qualitative measures used were the therapist's record of sessions and teacher survey. Efforts were made to make the drama therapy sessions and the measures used as naturalistic and as unobtrusive as possible so that the sessions were representative of the usual practice of the current drama therapist. The only unusual feature was the presence of the observer who was also familiar to the students and who remained as unobtrusive as possible.

Measures

Pre- and post-test

A pre- and post-test was carried out before and after the session to establish a baseline for attentiveness using an activity enjoyed by the individual student that did not require adult intervention. Ideally, each student is given an activity that is uniquely absorbing and pleasant for him. He would then be timed to see how long he is on task before adult intervention is required. However, in the current study, an identical activity was used for all the students. The reasons for this included the practicalities of the classroom where it was not possible to segregate the target students from the rest of the class. Second, the nature of the participants meant that it would have been difficult to offer a different activity to each student as this would have stimulated their curiosity and rivalry and thus increased distractibility. The teacher assessed the students immediately before and after the session to see whether their ability to focus on a task without adult intervention had improved. Each task comprised a paper and pencil activity involving colouring in and tracing letters. The teacher kept a concise, descriptive record of each student and his attention to the task over a five-minute period.

Observation record

The purpose of the observation record was to assess the attentiveness of the students during the drama therapy session. A ten-minute observation record was taken in the middle of the session by an independent observer who was experienced in making sample observations in a time interval observation schedule. The middle ten-minute section of the session was chosen to standardize the observation sampling procedure. The beginnings and endings of sessions were avoided, as attention was more variable at these times due to the anxiety around transitions felt by several of the students. This was borne out in one session where the observer inadvertently observed the final ten minutes of the session and two students were momentarily off task. Each of the target students was observed in turn at 15-second intervals for ten samples per session. The observer made a judgement of whether the student was on task based on his visual tracking and following of events in the session and participating in whatever the task was at the time. The number of on-task intervals were totalled and divided by the total possible number of intervals to establish a percentage on-task rate per session and an average over all six sessions.

Therapist record

Immediately after each session, the therapist took notes of how long each student focused on the activity and when he became distracted.

Teacher survey

The teacher was interviewed after each session in order to get additional information on her observations of the attentiveness of the four target students and other factors relevant to the study.

Instructional procedure

The programme consisted of weekly sessions of 35 minutes duration over six weeks. These were integrated into the regular classroom timetable. All children took part in the pre- and post-tests and the drama therapy sessions. The pre-test was administered directly after morning tea. It was referred to as 'work' and appeared thus on the timetable board which consisted of visual cue cards laminated and fixed to a board. The timetable board assisted students who benefited from a predictable routine and helped them prepare for whatever activity came next. During each session, an independent observer recorded the behaviour of the four target students for their level of attentiveness for a period of ten minutes in the middle of the session. The post-test took place immediately the drama session was over. This was also referred to as 'work' and appeared on the timetable board as such.

Programme support

Programme support beyond the drama therapist consisted of the class teacher and two teacher aides. The teacher was highly trained and experienced in special education. She was familiar with the students, as was one of the teacher aides. During the sessions, their roles were to model tasks for the students as requested by the therapist and manage behaviour where appropriate.

Results: therapist's record of sessions

Session one

The first session was the first experience of drama therapy for one of the target students so elements were introduced gradually to support him into a new process and assess his reaction.

WARM-UP

When everyone was seated, the therapist explained the presence of an observer and that 'we should pretend they are not here'. She greeted everyone individually with the 'Hello' song while the students clapped and waved. A group activity involving all the students was chosen to coincide with the entrance of the observer to lessen the chance of any one student becoming distracted. The activity chosen was playing with a length of lycra. The group began in a circle holding and pulling the lycra with both hands, and then lifting it up and down to create a breeze. The group then bounced a ball on the lycra and tried to see how long they could keep it from falling on the floor. Fine motor skills were used for gripping the lycra and gross motor skills for lifting the lycra in time with everyone in the group. Some students demonstrated good skills in this activity and attention and participation was good. As soon as interest began to wane, the therapist redirected the activity. Students took turns in pairs to go under the lycra while the others stretched it over them. The therapist encouraged exploratory touching and looking at shapes made by a pair of students under the lycra. It was at this point that the observer quietly entered the room but no one noticed as all the students were intent on stretching the lycra over their classmates to see what interesting bumps and textures were created. All students, even Steven (who was new to the class), were happy to wait their turn and help to stretch the lycra for the others. The therapist reiterated the familiar phrase, 'Everyone has a turn who wants a turn.' The therapist and support staff encouraged others to stay on task with phrases like 'good waiting'. Once each student had a turn, the therapist directed him back to his seat. When all students had had a turn, she began the story.

MAIN EVENT

The therapist explained that the story took place in the bush or forest. She asked if anyone knew any animals from the bush. The responses were slow in coming and varied in accuracy. The therapist produced a bag that was a familiar feature of the sessions. There was very good attention at this point. The therapist produced a collection of masks and props of butterflies, birds and bees. She asked the students to name the creatures as she held the props up. Two students named the masks correctly but all the students were watching intently. The therapist asked for sounds that could accompany the masks. She placed the props on the floor and asked each student what they would like to try. Support staff helped with any practical difficulties but most of the group were able to put on their own mask. The therapist encouraged sounds and movements to go with the mask or costume in order to facilitate the taking on of roles. All students participated fully and moved in role around the space in the middle of the circle of chairs. There was a minimum of structure and adult supervision while the students interacted with one another in role. The therapist requested a change of prop every few minutes so that everyone could have a turn. Students surrendered their masks without problems and shared with others. The therapist and staff reinforced appropriate behaviour with 'good sharing' or 'good listening'.

CLOSURE

The therapist nominated a staff member to collect props and requested students to return to their seats. She reinforced behaviour with 'good sitting'. She asked students to identify their favourite prop. Most of the students went to point or pick up the prop but all identified a favourite. The therapist explained that all these small creatures would be the characters explored in the story next week. The session ended with the 'Goodbye' song and students were ushered to their tables immediately in order to complete the post-test.

Session two

WARM-UP

This session began in the same way as the first with the 'Hello' song and a reminder of the presence of the observer. The therapist asked if anyone remembered any of the creatures from the previous week. The responses were slow and visual cues (the masks) were needed to elicit replies. The therapist introduced the character of Rata who went into the bush to chop down a tree to make a waka or boat. The therapist introduced the task, which involved a plastic axe and a cardboard box. She asked students to identify the prop. Several students put up their hands. The most accurate answer was 'chopper'. The therapist demonstrated the task, which involved holding the axe with both hands and chopping on the cardboard box with a 'one–two–three–stop' rhythm. The action was accompanied by the word 'chop' and followed by 'good chopping!' All the students were fully on task at this point and several immediately called out to have a turn. The therapist encouraged students to put up their hands and reminded them that 'everyone has a turn, who wants a turn'. All of the target students completed the task without any assistance from support staff. All the students clearly enjoyed the opportunity to wield the axe but did so within the parameters laid down by the therapist. They all also watched each other attentively and without any apparent loss of interest.

MAIN EVENT

The therapist reminded the students of the narrative: 'Rata went into the forest to find a tree to chop down to make a waka or boat.' The therapist asked for the assistance of a teacher aide to role-play the tree. She instructed her to wear a green tube of fabric and extend her arms. She modelled the task for the students, which involved swinging the axe at the base of the 'tree' (the bottom of the teacher aide's legs) but stopping just short of contact. The action was accompanied by a loud 'chop!' The therapist asked the teacher aide to react to 'blows' with an 'ouch' and begin to fall.

It took four chops to fell the tree. All the students giggled at the sounds of the 'tree' and got very excited when it toppled over. The therapist asked, 'Do you think I am hurting Lyn?' All the students replied, 'No,' or shook their heads. The therapist asked, 'Why is this not hurting Lyn?' Several students got out of their chairs to point at Lyn's legs where contact is not made. Satisfied that no one was under the illusion that the task was to hit the teacher aide, the therapist asked, 'Who wants a turn?' Several students put up their hands and the therapist chose Tom who was the most likely to give an accurate imitation. Tom copied the task perfectly even down to mimicking the therapist's vocal sounds as she hefted the axe. He smiled broadly when the 'tree' toppled and carefully took the axe and chopped off the smaller branches.

One student needed some physical support to hold the axe properly, but all took great care not to hit the teacher aide. Once the last student had a turn, the therapist returned to the animal masks and asked who wanted to play which animal. The masks were shared without a problem. The students were told to hide behind the chairs and wait. The therapist assumed the role of Rata finishing chopping down the tree and said, 'I am very hot (mimes) and tired (mimes) and thirsty (mimes) so I am going home for my dinner. I will be back tomorrow to carve my waka out of this tree.'

The therapist exited the stage area and support staff encouraged the students to help put the tree back up. Two students were very active in this, grabbed the 'tree', and pulled. All were very engaged in this activity. The students cheered when the tree stood upright and the two students who had been very involved earlier helped to pat down the 'roots' and replaced the woodchips.

The therapist returned as Rata and the students hid behind the chairs. The students laughed and giggled a lot when Rata reacted with amazement. He chopped down the tree again and left. The students re-entered the space and again helped the tree back into an upright position. This time more of the group actively participated.

The third time Rata hid and waited to see who was restoring the tree. He jumped out when the students came to help the tree and there was much shrieking and excitement. The therapist stopped the story at this point and explained that it was time to finish the session but 'we will find out what happens next session'.

CLOSURE

The therapist led the students in a de-role where they took off their mask and put it in the bag. Everyone sang the 'Goodbye' song.

Session three

WARM-UP

The session began as usual with a reminder about the observer and the 'Hello' song. The therapist reminded the students that the story took place in the bush and there were many creatures. She asked, 'Who remembers what they were?' Several students put up their hands. There were several correct answers and more recall than the previous week. The therapist said, 'Rata went into the forest to chop down a tree. What was he going to make with that tree?' One student called out, 'A boat,' while another student answered, 'Waka.'

The therapist introduced the task by saying, 'Today we are going to meet a very special person in the forest. He is Tane, god of the forest, and this is his costume.' The therapist put on the costume, which consisted of a brightly coloured feathered mask and a bright red cloak. She stood on a chair, looked slowly around the circle and bowed. All the students gazed at the therapist intently. The therapist de-roled by taking off the costume and mask and speaking in her normal voice. She asked, 'Who wants a turn?' One student needed some teacher support to get on the chair and maintain her balance while bowing but all were keen to participate and almost all maintained some degree of stillness in the role.

MAIN EVENT

The therapist returned to the narrative. She asked the same staff member to play the 'tree' and the students to role-play the creatures of the forest. The therapist playing Rata chopped down the tree for the third time but this time hid behind the desks and saw the 'creatures' helping the 'tree' back up. She rushed in and called out, 'Stop!' and claimed the tree was hers. The teacher supported the students to ask Rata if she has asked permission to take the tree. Rata asked, 'Whom should I ask?' The teacher supported Anne to say, 'Tane'. The therapist came out of role briefly to ask who wanted to play Tane. Steven volunteered straightaway. The teacher aide helped him into costume and onto the chair and Rata went down on his knees to ask, 'Please could I have this tree to make a waka?' Several of the other students shook their heads. Rata implored Tane, 'Please, can you help me? Can I have this tree?' Tane bowed his head very slowly as per the rehearsal and Rata said, 'Thank you, thank you.'

The therapist came out of role as Rata and said to the students, 'Now that Rata has asked permission, all the little creatures decide to help Rata carve his waka and they get down to scoop the wood.' The therapist modelled scooping with both hands on the body of the 'tree'. The staff member then sat up to be the head of the waka and the students were instructed to get in behind her one by one, with their arms around the waist of the person in front. The group sang 'Te waka' (a Maori song) and 'Row, row, row the boat' while they rocked from side to side. After they finished the song, they got out of the boat one by one in reverse order.

CLOSURE

Everyone returned their props to the bag and sat down. The therapist briefly summed up the whole story and the importance of asking permission before taking things. The group sang the 'Goodbye' song and finished.

Session four
WARM-UP

The session began as usual with the 'Hello' song and then the therapist briefly introduced the story of Paikea and the whale. She described the story as taking place on and in the sea. She asked the students, 'Who lives in the sea?' There were far more responses to this question than the previous sessions which focused on the forest or bush. Tom said 'fish' straightaway. Other suggestions were 'shark', 'snapper' and 'dolphin'.

The therapist asked who knew how to swim. Two students put up their hands immediately and one student began to demonstrate. The therapist asked the class to show her how they swam while sitting on their chairs, first using their arms and then their legs. The therapist took the bright blue lycra out of the bag and explained that she needed to see how the students swam on the lycra. She laid it on the floor and asked the teacher to demonstrate. The group stood and held the lycra to provide a surround for her while she mimed swimming. The students were delighted to see their teacher 'swimming'. Tom jumped up and down but still kept hold of the lycra and Anne was giggling.

The therapist asked, 'Who wants a turn?' Four of the students offered and the therapist chose Tom who demonstrated the task perfectly. All the students had a go. David was the last to offer but he did put up his hand with only a minimal prompt (a questioning look from support staff). The observer entered unnoticed by the students.

MAIN EVENT

The therapist asked the students to return to their seats. She explained that the story was about two brothers, a nice brother, Paikea, and a mean brother, Rahutapu. She demonstrated a 'mean' face and asked the students to copy. Anne and Steven did very 'mean' faces and were praised by the teacher. Tom stood with his hands on his hips and adopted a 'mean' posture that assisted him to alter his facial expression. David altered his facial expression but had trouble getting it to convey 'mean' or grumpy. All efforts were praised.

The therapist then took out the 'prop', which was a broom handle. She explained that Rahutapu, the 'mean' brother, built a beautiful waka and invited his brother Paikea to help him take it out to sea. They paddled the waka together. The therapist demonstrated how to hold the broom handle like a paddle. She showed the students how to paddle from side to side while making a swishing sound with her mouth. She asked, 'Who would like to go first?' Steven put up his hand. He sat on the stool and held the paddle correctly. When he moved the paddle from side to side the therapist pushed the stool he was sitting on and made the swishing sound. When he stopped paddling, the therapist stopped pushing the stool. The teacher said, 'It will only move while you paddle, Steven.'

Steven started to paddle again and the therapist pushed him fast. She took him round in a circle and back to the front of the group. Steven was smiling broadly as everyone clapped. The therapist praised Steven's paddling. She asked, 'Who is next?' Surprisingly, Anne, who usually waited longer while she watched the others, offered to go next. All of the students had a turn and David put up his hand without prompting.

The therapist asked, 'What is the swishing sound?' Tom said, 'The sea!' The therapist explained that in the story, Paikea falls out of the boat, so we need to practise our swimming again. She took a prop from the bag for the students to crawl through. It was a long narrow tube of fabric that support staff held at both ends. Steven and Tom jumped up and down on their seats with excitement. All the students were familiar with this from their sessions with a physiotherapist and they clearly enjoyed it. The therapist explained how to take a big breath before diving into the fabric. She asked, 'Who wants to go first?' Again, Anne was quick to volunteer. The teacher commented that Anne loved swimming and was very confident in the water. Anne remembered to take a big breath before she began crawling through the tube. One student needed support in order to get into a crawling position initially, but then managed without further support. Steven and Tom both wanted another turn but there was insufficient time.

CLOSURE

The fabric tube was returned to the bag. The group sang the 'Goodbye' song.

Session five
WARM-UP

The group sang the 'Hello' song and the therapist reiterated the story thus far. She asked again, 'Who lives in the sea?' Steven said, 'boats' and the teacher agreed that people can live on the water. There were a lot more suggestions of different kinds of fish including clown fish and puffer fish. The teacher explained that the class had been watching a video of the film 'Finding Nemo' that seemed to have influenced their suggestions.

MAIN EVENT

The therapist explained that the previous week we had practised paddling but it was easy because we had been in very calm water whereas this week we had to try paddling in rough water. The prop was the wobble board, which is a piece of wood on rockers with handles on either side. The therapist demonstrated sitting on the board and paddling while support staff rocked the board up and down. She asked for volunteers and Steven offered. From being quite watchful in the first few sessions when he was the 'new' boy, Steven now often took the lead in situations requiring physical aptitude.

The students were delighted to watch each person's efforts to stay on the board and everyone was keen to take part. The therapist moderated the rocking for less physically able or more timid students. The observer entered unnoticed at this time.

When everyone had had a turn, the therapist demonstrated falling out of the 'boat' (the wobble board) and explained its context in the story. Rahutapu, the mean brother, hated Paikea so much that he wanted to kill him so he removed the bung from the boat to make it sink, hoping to drown Paikea.

The therapist sat on the wobble board without a paddle but held the handles on either side. She rocked the wobble board three times looking increasingly startled and then mimed falling out of the boat with a loud 'aaaaargh'. She then mimed swimming desperately up for air. All the students watched the action intently. They giggled when the therapist rocked the wobble board and David clapped his hands when she fell out of the boat.

As each student had a turn, they anticipated the action more and by the final student all were counting and making the falling cry at the same time. One student was physically supported to fall out of the boat, but clearly enjoyed the opportunity and the subsequent swimming.

CLOSURE

The therapist put the prop in the bag and explained that next week they were going to find out who saved Paikea from drowning. The group sang the 'Goodbye' song and the session finished.

Session six
WARM-UP

The therapist entered with an inflatable whale, so all the students were very excited at the outset and wanted to touch and look at it. The therapist explained that everyone could have a turn in the session. The session began as usual with the 'Hello' song. The therapist asked what people could remember from the previous session. Steven said the whale and the therapist said, 'We haven't met the whale before but we talked about other creatures in the ocean.' Three of the students made suggestions, including David who had not verbalized an answer before.

The therapist returned to the story. She said there were two brothers and one was nice, 'and the other was...?' Tom said 'grumpy' and made a grumpy face. The therapist reminded the students that the two brothers went out in the waka and the mean brother took out the bung so that the boat began to sink. She asked if anyone remembered what happened next. Steven put up his hand and made the 'aaaargh' sound from the previous week. Everyone laughed and the therapist said 'That's right! Paikea fell out of the water into the deep ocean and he was in big trouble but someone came to help him.' She took out the inflatable whale and showed the group.

MAIN EVENT

Several students jumped up; the teacher reminded them to sit on their chairs, and that the whale would come round. The therapist passed the whale around the group so that each student could feel and look at it. She encouraged the students to pretend that it was a real animal. Steven laughed and mimed hitting the whale. The therapist said, 'No, Steven, be gentle.' The rest of the students were very gentle and respectful with the prop.

The therapist asked, 'Does anyone know how to ride a whale?' Several hands went up in response. The therapist said, 'I am going to show you the right way to ride the whale.' She demonstrated sitting astride the whale, leaning forward with her whole body in contact with the whale, holding on to the handles. She rocked the whale back and forth and then took care sliding off the whale 'as it swam into shallow water'. She said, 'Thank you,' to the whale. All the students participated enthusiastically. Once they were seated correctly, the therapist took the front of the inflatable and held the student steady while she rocked it back and forth. If students were not seated correctly, they had difficulty staying on.

Steven and Tom wanted another turn. Anne clearly loved it and David volunteered to have a turn without prompting, although he needed some support to sit in the correct position. Tom remembered to say 'Thank you' to the whale. Other students needed reminding. When everyone had had a turn, they were requested to return to their seats.

CLOSURE

The therapist summed up the story, saying, 'Paikea went on to become chief of the village. And his mean brother was never heard of again. Whenever we see a whale we should remember to say, "Thank you." And that was the end of the story.' The session ended with the packing up of the bag and the 'Goodbye' song.

Teacher interviews

The class teacher was interviewed after each session and completion of the post-test activity. As the time on task was nearly 100 per cent for all four target students, some of the structured interview ceased to be relevant. Consequently, questions became more general as to what the teacher thought were the greatest benefits of participating in sessions for the students. The major theme that arose from discussions with the class teacher was the acquisition and practising of social skills. A transcript of her comments is as follows:

> Children at this age are naturally egocentric and it is difficult for them to take turns and attend to others. You can try and teach them about taking part, but it's hard work and these children need it going over again and again.

Play is a good way to teach the different levels of standing back or moving forward, but the playground is less contained and you have to grab them at the time to get them to understand what's happening. Whereas in drama it's contained. You can slow it all down and concentrate on teaching one skill, like sharing the props, over and over. And they're having fun.

Both Steven and Tom are very energetic and full on, but I saw them beginning to stand back to let others move forward. Steven can be quite pushy and attention seeking but he learned quickly to participate without being silly. It also really seemed to stimulate his verbals. Tom was funny because he would mention the sessions a few days later. For example, we were having a session with the physiotherapist and she was getting them to crawl through the tunnel and he said, 'Swimming' which is what we had pretended it was in drama.

Anne can be quite moody, but even if she was in a mood before the session, she seemed to snap right out of it. I can see the way drama would be very important for someone like David as he is so shy and withdrawn and drama gets him to interact with the others. Gradually, they are all starting to interact like little kids do and starting to play with each other which is what we want.

Therapist's record of changes in the four target students

Steven

Steven was new to the school and drama therapy in Session one. He began by being very watchful and standing back, although quite willing to participate when it was his turn. He changed his position a few times in the group activity with the lycra, but seemed just to be wanting to get a better look. The teacher aide was vigilant as Steven had a tendency to push other children, but he did not physically touch anyone else during the sessions.

By Session two, he seemed a lot more relaxed, sitting nicely in his seat and paying attention. He began to put up his hand to volunteer, as the format started to become more familiar to him, and by Session three, he was eager to volunteer for everything.

Before the beginning of Session four, he seemed quite agitated and was striking poses and laughing, but as soon as we were seated and the song began, he calmed down and interacted appropriately for the rest of the session. He seemed to particularly enjoy the performing element and relished being centre stage. However, he always paid good attention to others having their turn.

Tom

Tom was agitated in Session one when the timetable board had not been changed to signal drama. He seemed very distracted in the 'Hello' song and as soon as it finished he leapt up to change the board. He stood up and flapped his hands for a few seconds but was still watching what I was doing. He announced what he had done and when this was acknowledged by the teacher he returned to his seat and became very attentive.

He enjoyed the physical aspects of the sessions and was always the first to volunteer to have a turn. Yet he seemed to appreciate the more imaginative, abstract elements. When he wore the animal masks, he made the appropriate movements and sounds to go with them.

He correctly identified the swishing sounds I made as we were paddling our waka as the sounds of the sea. Responding to the description of 'Rahutapu' as mean he put his hands on his hips and scowled for several seconds. He was also one of the students who appeared the most concerned about the welfare of the 'tree' in the story of Rata. He enthusiastically helped the 'tree' on every occasion and was very gentle and solicitous.

Anne

Anne became visibly more confident, physically and emotionally, over the course of the six sessions. She had problems with both her sight and her hearing and her balance was not good, but in all the physical activities she responded enthusiastically to the challenges and performed really well. She resisted attempts to help her and wanted to do things herself.

In Session one, she was very quiet so was encouraged to speak as she does have the ability to construct short sentences. By the end of Session three, she was able to attempt the line 'Please, can I have the tree?' At the end of Session six, her 'thank you' to the whale was loud and distinct.

Anne had been the focus of some bullying by another child in the class, and in the playground she often got upset and tearful. She began Session four still visibly upset from an altercation at morning tea. A lot of effort was made by staff to maintain distance between her and the other student, but with the high levels of interaction in drama it was not possible to maintain distance all of the time. However, on the couple of occasions when they did have contact, Anne was very assertive with this student and did not seem unduly fazed. The majority of the time, Anne interacted with the other students in a positive way, sharing props and taking turns.

David

David tended to be very shy and passive but this improved over the course of the sessions. We deliberately reduced the amount of support that was given to encourage him to participate. In Session one, the therapist asked him if he wanted to participate when she saw him looking at her very intently. In Session two, the teacher aide gave him a gentle nudge to put up his hand and offer to have a go. By Session six, he was raising his hand of his own accord when the therapist very pointedly said, 'Raise your hand if you want a turn.' He participated even when he felt shy being in front of the group and the centre of attention.

In Session five, the task was to sit on the wobble board boat while it was rocked and then fall off in slow motion into the 'sea'. David did the task perfectly, with his eyes tightly shut and blushing. He smiled and opened his eyes when he was given a round of applause.

David could be inattentive in class and because he is very quiet it could go unnoticed. However, in drama, he was given so many opportunities to participate and his attention was demanded so often (the therapist would ask him a question if his eyes looked unfocused) that he was observed being briefly off task on only four occasions.

Pre- and post-test

The pre- and post-test activity was used to assess whether participation in drama therapy sessions influenced attentiveness levels in the target students after the session compared with before the session. Two of the students averaged similar levels on task both before the intervention and afterwards. Further, one student scored more and one student scored less time on task after the intervention compared with before the intervention.

Observation record

For three out of the six sessions the target students were 100 per cent on task for the ten-minute period in which they were observed. Of the remaining three sessions, there were a few exceptions. In Session two, the observation period occurred in the final ten minutes of the session instead of the middle period. Two of the target students were observed off task as the 'Goodbye' song was signalling the end of the session. One of these students, David, was observed being off task briefly in the middle of Session two and at the end of Session four. Steven was observed off task in the middle of Session six.

Summary

Changes were observed in the four target students over the course of the six sessions. The two most outgoing students learned to temper their enthusiasm to participate with a greater regard for their less extrovert classmates. The physically under-confident student learned to take risks, knowing and trusting the therapist and the ritual of the sessions. The shy and withdrawn student began to volunteer and speak up more. These results were expected because the sessions combined an enjoyable, developmentally appropriate medium with a familiar, consistent structure where the guidelines for participating were regularly reinforced.

Conclusion

Four students took part in six sessions of drama therapy. The pre- and post-test indicated little variation in their attention levels before and after the intervention. The observation schedule indicated that all of the students paid attention for the majority of the observation time despite interruptions and distractions such as the entrance of the observer. The therapist record and comments from the teacher described how they practised social skills such as listening to others, taking the lead and taking part in cooperative group endeavours through their active participation in drama therapy sessions.

Teachers and other professionals at the school often remarked on the levels of attentiveness of these students when they observed drama therapy sessions. This study aimed to both check these observations and explore whether participation in drama therapy sessions improved attentiveness after the session and in other activities.

The current review of the literature showed that this was an area not well researched, although key elements of good teaching practice aligned well with specific features of the drama therapy session. These included the importance of using a variety of methods, making the session vivid and attractive to the senses and providing plenty of opportunities for students to actively participate in learning experiences and the use of traditional stories. The latter were used to provide the structure needed and the exciting, interactive material so engaging to the student.

Students with an intellectual disability have a variety of issues with which they have to deal educationally, socially and emotionally. Their cognitive abilities may be impaired by their inability to focus their attention in class. In the first years of school, the teacher aims to engage the students in learning as well as teach the rudiments of behaviour that should stand them in good stead throughout their school career. These include basic skills such as turn taking, sharing, sitting on the chair and staying on task. Often students with an intellectual disability can settle to a task with one-on-one adult supervision, but find interacting with their peers in groups more challenging. The drama therapy group is an ideal situation to learn the self-mastery skills of being able to focus attention in the midst of many distractions and others competing for attention.

This research study, though of a short duration and comprising a small number of participants, supported the value of this particular intervention with students with an intellectual disability. There are implications for its wider use not only in special schools but also in mainstream schools where there is a specific need. Its application to children and young people whose standard means of communication are through nonverbal means such as play or enactment cannot be underestimated.

References

Aldridge, D., Gustorff, D. and Neugebauer, L. (1995) 'A preliminary study of creative music therapy in the treatment of children with developmental delay.' *The Arts in Psychotherapy 22*, 3, 189–205.

Antia, S.D. and Kreimeyer, K.H (1992) 'Social competence intervention for young children with hearing impairments.' in S.L. Odom, S.R. McConnell and M.A. McEnvoy (eds) *Social Competence of Young Children with Disabilities: Issues and Strategies for Intervention.* Baltimore, MD: P.H. Brookes.

Attwood, T. (1998) *Asperger's Syndrome.* London: Jessica Kingsley Publishers.

BADth (British Association of Dramatherapists) (1998) Information pack. Available from The Secretary, 5 Sunnydale Villas, Durlston Road, Swanage, Dorset.

Bank-Mikkelson, N. (1969) 'A metropolitan area in Denmark: Copenhagen.' In R. Kugel and W. Wolfenberger (eds) *Issues in Special Education.* Mountain View, CA: Mayfield Publishing.

Berk, L.E. (1996) *Child Development.* Boston, MA: Allyn and Bacon.

Berrol, C. (1989) 'A view from Israel: Dance/movement and the creative arts therapies in special education.' *Arts in Psychotherapy 16*, 81–90.

Bettleheim, B. (1978) *The Uses of Enchantment.* London: Peregrine Books.

Blatner, A (1988) *Foundations of Psychodrama: History, Theory and Practice.* New York: Springer Publishing Co.

Boal, A. (1995) *The Rainbow of Desire.* London: Routledge.

Bortoli, A. and Brown, P. (2002) 'The social attention of children with disabilities during social engagement opportunities.' Unpublished Doctorate thesis. University of Melbourne: Australia. Further details available from Anna Bortoli, Early Intervention Unit, Department of Learning and Educational Development, The University of Melbourne, Parkville 3052, Australia.

Brophy, K. and Hancock, S. (1985) 'Adult–child interaction in an integrated preschool programme. Implications for teacher training.' *Early Child Development and Care 22*, 275–94.

Casson, John (1997) 'Dramatherapy history in headlines.' *Journal of the British Association for Dramatherapists 19*, 10–13.

Chesner, A. (1995) *Dramatherapy for People with Learning Disabilities.* London: Jessica Kingsley Publishers.

Cole, P. and Chan, L. (1990) *Methods and Strategies for Special Education.* Sydney: Prentice Hall.

Corey, G. and Corey, M. (1997) *Groups Process and Practice* (5th edn). Belmont, CA: Wadsworth Thomson Learning.

Craig, H.K. (1993) 'Social skills of children with specific language impairment: peer relationships.' *Language, Speech and Hearing Services in Schools 24*, 206–15.

Csoti, M. (2000) *People Skills for Young Adults.* London: Jessica Kingsley Publishers.

Dent-Brown, K. (1999) 'The six part story method as an aid in the assessment of personality disorder.' *Dramatherapy 21*, 2 (Autumn), 10–14.

Edwards, J. (1998) 'Strategies for living skills, strategies for meeting the needs of adolescents and adults'. In V. Omitriev and P. Oelwe (eds) *Advances in Down Syndrome.* Seattle: Special Child Publications.

Emunah, R. (1994) *Acting for Real: Drama Therapy Process, Technique, and Performance.* New York: Brunner/Mazel Publishers.

Erikson, E. (1995) *Childhood and Society.* London: Vintage.

Geldard, K. and Geldard, D. (2001) *Working with Children in Groups.* Hampshire: Palgrave.

Gersie, A. (1997) *Reflections on Therapeutic Storymaking.* London: Jessica Kingsley Publishers.

Goldstein, H., Kaczmarek, L. and English, K. (2002) *Promoting Social Communication*. Baltimore, MD: Paul. H. Brookes Publishing.

Hallahan, D. and Kauffman, J. (1978) *Exceptional Children*. New Jersey: Prentice-Hall.

Hartup, W.W. (1989) 'Social relationships and their developmental significance.' *American Psychologist 44*, 2, 120–6.

Hewett, F. and Forness, S. (1977) *Education of Exceptional Learners*. Boston, MA: Allyn and Bacon.

Jennings, S. (1973) *Remedial Drama*. London: A. and C. Black.

Jennings, S. (1990) *Dramatherapy with Families, Groups and Individuals*. London: Jessica Kingsley Publishers.

Jennings, S. (1992) *Dramatherapy Theory and Practice 2*. London: Routledge.

Jennings, S. (ed.) (1995) *Dramatherapy with Children and Adolescents*. London: Routledge.

Johnson, K. (1981) *Impro*. London: Methuen.

Johnson, L. and O'Neill, C. (eds) (1984) *Dorothy Heathcote: Collected Writings on Drama and Education*. London: Hutchinson and Co. Ltd.

Kasari, C., Freeman, S., Mundy, P. and Sigman, M.E. (1995) 'Attention regulation by children with Down syndrome.' *American Journal on Mental Retardation 100*, 2, 128–36.

King-Sears, M.E. (1997) 'Best academic practices for inclusive classrooms.' *Focus on Exceptional Children 29*, 7, 1–22.

Krakow, J. and Kopp, C.B. (1982) 'Sustained attention in young Down syndrome children.' *Topics in Early Childhood Special Education 2*, 2, 32–42.

Laban, R. (1980) *The Mastery of Movement* (4th edn). London: Macdonald and Evans.

Landy, R.J. (1986) *Dramatherapy: Concepts and Practices*. Springfield, IL: Charles C. Thomas.

Lavoie, R. (1994) *Social Development and Adolescence: Why Don't They Like Me?* Boston, MA: Woodbine House.

Little, L. (2002) 'Middle-class mothers' perceptions of peer and sibling victimization among children with Asperger's syndrome and non-verbal learning disorders issues.' *Comprehensive Paediatric Nursing 25*, 43–57.

Lyons, S. and Tropea, E. (1987) 'Creative arts therapists as consultants: methods and approaches to in-service training in the Special Education Forum.' *Arts in Psychotherapy 14*, 243–7.

Mailloux, Z. (1993) *Sensory Integration Quarterly*.

Oaklander, V. (1978) *Windows to Our Children*. Highland, NY: The Gestalt Journal Press.

O'Doherty, S. (1989) 'Play and drama therapy with the Down's syndrome child.' *Arts in Psychotherapy, 16*, 171–8.

Opie, I. and Opie, P. (1980) *The Classic Fairy Tales*. London: Paladin.

Orbell, M. (1992) *Traditional Maori Stories*. Auckland: Reed Publishing.

Pearson, J. (1996) *Discovering the Self through Movement and Drama*. London: Jessica Kingsley Publishers.

Rose-Krasnor, L. (1985) 'Observational assessment of social problem solving.' In B.H. Schneider, K.H. Rubin and J.E. Ledinghan (eds) *Children's Peer Relations: Issues in Assessment and Intervention*. New York: Springer-Verlag.

Ross, D.D. and Rogers, D.L. (1990) 'Social competence in kindergarten: analysis of social negotiations during peer play.' *Early Child Development and Care 64*, 15–26.

Roth, E. and Rowland, B. (1980) 'Parallels in art and play therapy with a disturbed retarded child.' *Arts in Psychotherapy 7*, 19–26.

Schumaker, J. and Deshler, D. (1995) 'Social skills and learning disabilities.' *Learning Disabilities Association of America Newsbriefs*, March–April. Available from www.ldonline.org/Ld_indepth/social_skills_and_ld.htm.

Shatner, G. and Courtney, R. (eds) (1997) *Drama in Therapy*, Vol. 1. New York: Drama Book Specialists.

Slade, P. (1968) *The Experience of Spontaneity*. London: Longman.

Slade, P. (1995) *Child Play: Its Importance for Human Development*. London: Jessica Kingsley Publishers.

Stanislavski, C. (1949) *An Actor Prepares*. New York: Theatre Arts.

Thompson, J. (1999) *Drama Workshops for Anger Management and Offending Behaviour.* London: Jessica Kingsley Publishers.

Thompson, M., O'Neill Grace, C. and Cohen, L. (2001) *Best Friends, Worst Enemies.* London: Penguin.

Tuhiwai-Smith, L. (1999) *Decolonizing Methodologies Research and Indigenous Peoples.* Dunedin, New Zealand: University of Otago Press.

Vygotsky, L. (1978) *Mind in Society: The Development of Higher Psychological Processes.* Cambridge, MA: Harvard University Press.

Warren, B. (1993) *Using the Creative Arts in Therapy.* London: Routledge.

Watts, P. (1985) 'Myth enactment.' *Educare,* June–Sept.

Watts, P. (1992) 'Therapy in Drama' in *Dramatherapy: Theory and Practice 2,* Sue Jennings (ed). London and New York: Routledge.

Weaver, B. (1996/7) 'A golden moment: dramatherapy and Peter Slade.' *Dramatherapy 18,* 3, 15–21.

Wengrower, H. (2001) 'Art therapies in educational settings: and intercultural encounter.' *Arts in Psychotherapy 28,* 109–15.

Westera, J. (2002) *Reciprocal teaching as a school-wide inclusive strategy.* Unpublished Doctorate thesis. New Zealand: University of Auckland.

Wood, J. and Lazari, A. (1997) *Exceeding the Boundaries. Understanding Exceptional Lives.* Fort Worth, TX: Harcourt Brace College.

Wilkinson, H. (1980) *Spontaneity and Imagination in Drama: An Investigation.* Victoria, Australia: Education Department of Victoria, Research and Development, Curriculum Branch.

Useful Websites

www.berattarverkstan.se/engindex.htm
www.folktale.net
www.mythfolklore.net/andrewlang
www.pitt.edu/~dash/folktexts.html
www.scbwi.org/pubs/scbwi_pubs/Children_Crisis.pdf
www.stavacademy.co.uk/mimir
www.storyarts.org
www.storyconnection.net
www.storydynamics.com
www.storyteller.net
www.storytellingpower.com
www.surlalunefairytales.com/index.html

Subject Index

Page numbers in italics refer to photographs.
Specific story titles have been grouped under the main heading stories.

absorption 20–1, 173–4
abuse 100–1
achievements 21
actions, learning about the consequences of 40, 159
ADHD *see* attention deficit hyperactivity disorder
adolescents 19
    with Asperger syndrome 162–4
    with attentional/ behavioural problems 157–62
    with intellectual disability 154–7
aesthetic space 178
affect, lack of 36
affirming behaviour 164
aggressive behaviour 24–5, 131
    habitual 25
    in response to unwanted physical proximity 24–5
alertness 173
allies, turning enemies into 122, 148
altruism 40, 58
American Association of Mental Retardation 11
animals
    masks 34, 47–8, 109, 183
    role-playing 47–8, 49, 53–4
    stories 46–50, 79–81, 115–19, 123–5, 190–1
anti-social behaviour 159–60
art therapy 14, 15, 16
Asperger syndrome 29, 125, 152
    adolescents with 162–4
    and competitiveness 135
    and consistency 135
    diagnostic criteria for 162
    and rule-fixation 135
    and victimisation 114
assertiveness 105, 154, 193–4
assessments
    of attention 180–2, 194, 195
    of group level 18–19
attention
    absorption 20–1, 173–4
    assessment 180–2, 194, 195
    definition 172
    divided 173
    engaging 12, 171–96
    focused 173
    importance of 171–2
    shifts in 172, 173
    sustained 173
attention deficit hyperactivity disorder (ADHD) 14, 29, 159
attention-seeking behaviour 25
autism 70, 125, 136
    and drama therapy participation 45–6
    masks and 35
    and movement with touch 61
    and the need for familiar structure 38
    and the need for personal space 25
    visual storyboards and 165–70
autism spectrum disorders 179
    and the need for routine 62
    Tom 179, 187–93
autocosmic play 18–19

babies, with special needs 100
BADth *see* British Association of Dramatherapists
ball games 161
'ball pools' 104
balloons 155
Beauty and the Beast 148
beauty walks 111–12
behavioural difficulties 15, 29
    see also aggressive behaviour
bells 49–50
benefits of drama therapy 13–14
best practice, teaching 175
betrayal 130
'better life, a', striving for 150–1
'boats' 127–8, 138–40, 188, 189
boundaries 48, 162
'bow wow' game 155
bows and arrows 133–4
British Association of Dramatherapists (BADth) 10, 173
'British bulldog' ('Bullrush') game 143–4
bullying 25–6, 131, 133, 193–4

carrying tasks 123
Cartesian dualism 28
case studies
    Anne (developmental delay) 179, 187–8, 191–4
    David (Down syndrome) 179, 187–92, 194–5
    Steven (Down syndrome) 179–80, 183, 188–93, 195

case studies cont.
Tom (autism spectrum disorder) 179,
187–93
cause and effect 127–8, 165
'caves', making 121–2
censorship 158–9
chairs
getting kids to sit on 18–20, 73
swapping games 65–6, 155
challenges, presenting 48
change
resistance to 62, 179
stories of 62–71
'change three things' task 163
chants 75–6
chases 43–4
child abuse 100–1
Chinese deluge myths 42
choice, offering 22–3, 36–7
Christianity 100
Christmas 100
class layout 20, 21, 178
classroom environments 19–21
'cliff top' game 161
climbing 59–60, 93
closure 176
examples 183–5, 187, 189–91
collaborative play 129
collectivism 28, 83
colour, working with 75, 76–7
communication skills training 15
competitiveness 129–40
conduct disorder 29, 89, 159–60
confidence
in students 26
of the therapist 26
conflict resolution 129
confrontation, avoidance 157
consequences, learning about 40, 159
consistency, need for 135
containment 122
control
feelings of 86
taking/abdicating 156
coordination tasks 127–8, 151
see also fine motor skills
'cornflakes' game 65–6, 155
creation myths 101, 109–13
creative thinking 64, 153, 154–5
cultural diversity 137–8, 177
cultural identity 27
culture of drama sessions 23–4

dance therapy 14–15, 16
defining drama therapy 9–11
developmental age 18
developmental play paradigm 18–19
*Diagnostic and Statistical Manual of Mental
Disorders*, Fourth Edition (DSM IV)
162
disguise 92–3
distancing techniques 28, 29, 133, 157
distractibility (under-attention) 172, 174,
176
diversionary tactics 153
dominance, group 127
Down syndrome 15–16, 101, 179–80
David 179, 187–92, 194–5
Steven 179–80, 183, 188–93, 195
dressing up 78, 92–3, 95–6, 125, 134,
144, 178
drug abuse 159
'duck, duck, goose' game 133

education 12
egocentricity 72, 191–2
embodiment stage 18–19
emotional safety 24, 25–6, 28
emotions
'lacking affect' 36
learning about through narrative 165–6
problems 15–16
'sculpting' 156, 162–3
Eris (Discord) 103
essential oils 70
exclusion from therapy 25
executive function 173

fabrics 33, 42, 108, 125, 187–9
Lycra 33, 68–9, 73–4, 182–3, 187
failure, fear of 158
fairies 149–53
falling, controlled 138–9
'farmer wants a wife' game 93
fearful children 98–9
fidgets 11
fine motor skills 133–4, 182
'fires' 152
'fishing' 149–53
foot massage 112
forgiveness 130
'freeze frames' technique 157
friendship 12–13, 111
future, visualisation of 159–60

generalization 154, 171
Gilgamesh 63
'grandmother's footsteps' game 95
grandparents 94–5, 103
greed 58, 129
Greek stories/traditions 103, 136, 142–4
gross motor skills 182
group status/dominance 127

hand dancing 71
hand massage 70
helping others, stories about 40–61, 80–4
here and now, fear of entering 158
heroes 83, 85, 92, 141
    super 108
    unlikely 92, 114–28
hide and seek 92
'hiding the bee' game 125
holistic approaches 14
horizontal relationships 72
'horse race' task 163
humanism 28
hyperactive children 23
    see also attention deficit hyperactivity
        disorder

identification 131–2
Ihimaera, Witi 137
impact of teaching material 174–5
impulse control 13, 88, 131
    in adolescents 159, 160
inattention 173
inclusive settings 72
individualism 83
infantile needs 121–2
interactive teaching methods 175
interconnectedness 58, 75

jealousy 130, 131–3
Jesus Christ 100
jewellery, costume 78
journeys 58–9, 60, 81–4, 118, 152

Laban body shapes 44–5
    ball 44
    pin 44
    twist 44, 45
    wall 44, 45
language
    absence 18–19
    acquisition 15
learning disability, definition of 11
'level of the group', assessment 18–19

lifting tasks 123
losing, perceived as life and death scenario
    135
Lycra 33, 68–9, 73–4, 182–3, 187

main events 176
    examples 183, 184–5, 186–7, 188–91
Maori stories/traditions 54, 63, 87, 94–5,
    126, 137–40
masks 34–5, 43, 174
    animal 34, 47–8, 109, 183
    scary 79, 97, 122
maturation 64–5
metamorphosis 104
metaphor 128, 129, 133, 135
miming 113, 156–7
mistakes, owning up to 124
mistrust 141
modelling 22, 177
    of gentle touch 74
monster stories 119–23
moon 77–8
motor skills
    see also coordination tasks
    fine 133–4, 182
    gross 182
'movement with touch' 60–1
movements, of the therapist 12
music therapy 14, 15, 16

'name two things' tasks 155
narrative 165–6
Native American Indian tradition 75, 84,
    97, 101, 111–12, 116, 133
natural world 80
neglect 100
nets, making 68
noise sensitivity 24
nourishment, inaccessible 64
numinous 101
nurturance 122

occupational therapists 20, 112
'Oranges and Lemons' rhyme/game 136–7
other people
    sense of 28
    stories about helping 40–61, 80–4
over-attention 172
over-sensitivity to information 172
Ovid 104

paddling exercise 127
participation see student participation

peer interaction 72, 73, 158, 196
'pegs' game 162
percussion 35, 42–4
performance anxiety 12
permission, asking for 51
perseveration 172
personal growth 40
personal play 36
personal space 25, 73
philosophy 28
physical proximity 24–5, 73–4
physical safety 24–6
physiotherapists 20, 112
'ping pong' game 162
'planting the seeds' exercise 45–6
play
    autocosmic 18–19
    collaborative 129
    personal 36
    projected 36
    special school playground 72–3
play therapy 15, 16
playdoh 117
post-traumatic stress disorder (PTSD) 29
posture 44–5, 156
'pots, making' 117
premature babies 131
pretence, lack of a concept of 170
projected play 36
proprioception 16, 48–9, 60, 123
props
    appealing 175, 177–8
    fabrics 33, 42, 68–9, 73–4, 108, 125,
        182–3, 187–9
    masks 34–5, 43, 47–8, 79, 97, 109,
        122, 174, 183
    practical examples of 45–9, 52–5,
        58–61, 65–6, 68–9, 73–6, 78–9,
        81, 83–4, 88, 92–3, 95–9, 104–5,
        108–9, 111–13, 117–19, 127–8,
        133–4, 136–40, 143–4, 148–9,
        151–3, 182–5, 188–91
    sensory nature of 174
proximal zone 30, 158
psychoanalysis 10
psychological aspects, of learning disability
    101–13
PTSD see post-traumatic stress disorder
pushing and pulling 60–1, 105
put-downs 25–6

qualitative data 180
quantitative data 180

rainbows 76–7
rainmakers 35, 84
Rapunzel 148
'red light/green light' ('stop 'n' go') game
    160–1
rejection 15
relationships
    horizontal 72
    peer interactions 72, 73, 158, 196
    vertical 72
relays 95–6
research study 171–96
    assessment of attention 180–2, 194,
        195
    design 180
    drama session components 176–80
    instructional procedure 181–2
    measures 180–1
    observation records 181, 194–5
    participants 179–80
    programme support 182
    results 182–92
    teacher surveys 181, 191–2
    therapist records 181, 182–91, 192–5
Ritalin 179
rites
    failure to observe 101–3, 136
    of passage 97
rivalry 130, 131
    see also sibling rivalry
role reversal 65
role-playing 22, 26, 36, 163
    animals 47–8, 49, 53–4
    trees 52–3
ropes 59–60, 93, 117–18, 161
routines 62
rules 135

safety 23–6, 122
    emotional 24, 25–6, 28
    physical 24–6
'scarves' game 122–3
scene setting 42–4
schizophrenia 160
'sculpting' technique 156, 162–3
'seed planting' exercise 45–6, 76
self, sense of 23, 37
self-consciousness 158
self-mastery skills 196
self-sacrifice 83
semi-circle class layout 20, 21, 178
sensory experience 174
sequences 31–2
Sesame approach 13

Sesame Institute 10
sexual maturation 64–5
shape shifting 96–7, 102
sharing 129
'sharks and islands' game 162
sibling rivalry 102, 103, 127, 138
single parents 92
Sleeping Beauty 103
social competence 12, 72
social skills practice 12–15, 73–4, 129,
    191, 195
social stories 154
songs 37–8, 42, 118–19, 139–40
    for beauty walks 111–12
    examples 49–50, 54–5, 68, 76–7, 79,
        84, 104–5, 108–9
    'Oranges and Lemons' rhyme/game
        136–7
space
    aesthetic 178
    of the classroom 19–21
    personal 25, 73
    of the session 19–20, 21, 178
'special child' stories 100–13
speech and language therapists 139, 148
'spider webs', making 117–18
spontaneity 154–5
stasis 63
status, group 127
stereotypic behaviours 62
stories 16
    see also traditional stories
    adolescents and 19
    Atalanta and the golden apples 134–7
    about change 62–71
    about competitiveness 129–40
    devising your own 154–64
    Grandmother spider 115–19
    about helping others 40–61, 80–4
    Hemi and the whale 79–81
    Jack and the Beanstalk 85, 89–93
    Kahakura 142, 149–53
    King Arthur's gold 85, 86–9
    Maui and the sun 30–1, 62, 66–9
    Maui's search for fire 85, 93–6
    Momotaro 31, 101, 103, 105–9
    Morning star, evening star 101, 109–13
    Paikea 137–40, 187–91
    Psyche and Amor 35, 141, 142–4
    Rata the wanderer 40, 50–5, 58,
        184–7, 193
    Raven and the giant who sits on the
        tide 62, 63–6
    Raven and the light 85, 86, 96–9

Solomon and the bee 123–5
about 'special children' 100–13
structure of 11, 27, 176
Tarantula and swift runner 129–34
tasks of the 43–5, 177
about team working 72–84, 111
The bell of Hamana 46–50, 58, 166–9,
    167-9
The birth of Maui 101–5
The bog people 77–9
The children and the thunder god
    31–2, 41–6
The first sail 125–8
The healing waters 81–4
The thunder of the four colours 74–7
The umbrella tree 55–61
The Windmaker 62–3, 69–71
about trickery and stealing 85–99
about trust 141–53
types of 11
about unlikely heroes 92, 114–28
Vassilisa and Baby Yaga Bony Legs
    141–2, 144–9
Yukos and the monster 119–21
storms, scene setting 42–4
storyboards, visual 165–70, 167-9
storytelling 9, 39
structure
    of drama sessions 38–9, 71, 176
    need for in autism 38
    of stories 11, 27, 176
student participation 31–2, 36–9, 43–5
    freedom of 12
superheroes 108
support 141, 143
support staff 178
    in action 182, 183, 184–5, 186–7
    creating trust 141
    encouraging physical safety 24–5
    training for 21–3
Swiss balls 65–6, 68–9, 109
sword play/fighting 88–9

'tag' game 143–4
tasks of the story 43–5, 177
teachers
    enthusiasm of 21
    surveys 181, 191–2
teaching
    adaptations 175
    best practice 175
team working 72–84, 111
tents 97–8

themes in stories 176, 177
    change 64–5, 67–8, 70
    competitiveness 131–3, 135–6, 137–8
    helping others 42, 47, 51, 58, 80, 83
    'special children' 103, 108, 111
    team working 75, 78, 80, 83
    trickery and stealing 92, 94–5, 97
    trust 141–2, 148, 150–1
    the unlikely hero 116, 121, 124, 127
therapeutic environment 23–4, 178
therapist records 181, 182–91, 192–5
thunder 42, 113
time-out chair 25
touch, gentle 74
traditional stories 27–39
    see also stories
    action content 29–30, 36
    audiences for 29
    choosing 29–32
    experience affirming 27
    finding 32
    indirect nature of 27–8
    Maui and the sun 30–1, 62, 66–9
    Momotaro 31, 101, 103, 105–9
    props for 32–5, 39
    reasons for using 27–9, 176–8
    relevance to students 177
    resources of 27
    and role allocation 36–7
    sequences of 31–2
    and session structure 38–9
    six-stages of 30–1
    use of song 37–8
    storytelling process 39
    structure 11, 27, 29, 176
    student participation/interaction 31–2,
        36–9
    tasks of 31–2, 39
    The children and the thunder god
        31–2, 41–6
transformation 75
trickery and stealing, stories about 85–99,
    135
true worth, appreciation of 128
trust
    atmospheres of 141
    stories of 141–53
tubes, fabric 33, 188–9
tug-of-wars 161
turn-taking 23, 149, 191–2

under-attention (distractibility) 172, 174,
    176
underdog theme 92, 114–28

ungrounded students 111
unloved, feeling 132–3

VAKT (visual, auditory, kinaesthetic and
    tactile) method 174
vertical relationships 72
victimisation 114
visual learners 22
visual storyboards 165-70, 167-9
voice 12, 105
vulnerability 26

warm-up exercises 155, 176
    for adolescent groups 160–2, 163–4
    examples 182–7, 189–90
water, representations of 108, 187–9
weather, scene setting 42–4, 83, 113, 128
Western philosophy 28
'What's the time, Mister Wolf?' game 113
wheel-chair bound students 22–3, 33, 43,
    45, 59, 59–60, 68, 112
will 61, 67–8, 105
wind 128
'wind, tree, cow' task 163–4
windmakers 70
wobble boards 138–9, 189–90, 194

Author Index

Aldridge, D. 14, 15, 16
Antia, S.D. 12
Attwood, T. 62, 135

Bank-Mikkelson, N. 60
Beirne-Smith 172
Berk, L.E. 12
Berrol, C. 14–15, 16
Bettleheim, B. 114
Boal, A. 178
Bortoli, A. 38, 172–3
Brophy, K. 72
Brown, P. 38, 172–3

Casson, J. 10
Chan, L. 12, 175
Chesner, A. 13–14, 16, 23, 26, 72, 154, 165
Cohen, L. 129
Cole, P. 12, 175
Corey, G. 13
Corey, M. 13
Craig, H.K. 12
Cruikshank 174
Csoti, M. 12, 154

Dent-Brown, K. 28
Descartes, R. 28
Deshler, D. 13
Douglas 38, 172
Durell 177

Edwards, J. 72
Emunah, R. 10, 178
Erikson, E. 18, 141

Fernald 174
Forness, S. 172, 174
Freud, S. 10

Geldard, D. 13
Geldard, K. 13
Gersie, A. 177
Goforth 177
Gustorff, D. 14, 16

Hallahan, D. 174
Hancock, S. 72

Hartup, W.W. 72
Hewett, F. 172, 174

Jennings, S. 10, 13, 18, 30, 154
Johnson, K. 155
Jung, C.G. 10, 101

Kasari, C. 172
Kauffman, J. 174
Keogh 38, 172
King-Sears, M.E. 175
Kopp 38, 172
Kopp, C.B. 12
Krakow, J. 12
Kreimeyer, K.H. 12
Kymissus 13

Laban, R. 10
Lahad, M. 30
Landy, R.J. 158
Lavoie, R. 12–13
Lazari, A. 172, 175
Lindvist, M. 10, 13, 60–1
Little, L. 114
Lyons, S. 14

Mailloux, Z. 48
Margolis 38, 172
Moreno 10

Neugebauer, L. 14, 16
Nordoff 14

Oaklander, V. 23, 37
O'Doherty, S. 15–16
O'Neill Grace, C. 129
Opie, I. 92
Opie, P. 92
Orbell, M. 176

Palincsar 175
Patton 172
Payne 172
Pearson 61
Piaget, J. 73

Richman, M. 14
Robbins 14
Rogers, D.L. 12
Rose-Krasnor, L. 12
Ross, D.D. 12

Roth, E. 15
Rothbart 172–3
Rowland, B. 15
Ruff 172–3

Sachs 177
Schumaker, J. 13
Semrud-Clikeman 38, 172
Slade, P. 10, 20, 36, 173
Spillmann 177
Stanislavski, C. 158
Strauss 174

Teeter 38, 172
Thompson, J. 162
Thompson, M. 129
Tropea, E. 14
Tuhiwai-Smith, L. 28

Vaughn 38, 172
Vygotsky, L. 30, 158

Warren, B. 26
Watts, P. 27, 28, 36
Weaver, B. 173
Wengrower, H. 14, 16
Werner 174
Westera, J. 175
Wilkinson, H. 158
Wood, J. 172, 175

18570763R00111

Made in the USA
Lexington, KY
13 November 2012